" WHAT I LEARNED LATER IN LIFE, TOO LATE, IS THAT WHEN YOU HAVE POWER OVER ANOTHER PERSON, ASKING THEM TO LOOK AT YOUR D...K ISN'T A QUESTION. IT'S A PREDICAMENT FOR THEM."

—LOUIS C.K.

REALITYCOVERBOOKS.COM

STARTING AT THE TOP!

A Who's Who of the Accused

Donald Gorbach

ISBN-10 1981807462
ISBN-13 978-1981807468

BILL CLINTON
42nd President of the United States

GEORGE H.W. BUSH
41st President of the United States

DONALD J. TRUMP
45th President of the United States

ROGER AILES
Former Chairman and CEO of Fox News

ANDRE BALAZS
Hotelier

JOHN BESH
Celebrity Chef

LOUIS C.K.
Comedian

JOHN CONYERS
U.S. Congressman

ANDY DICK
Actor/Comedian

RICHARD DREYFUSS
Actor

MICHAEL ORESKES
Former NPR News Chief

JEREMY PIVEN
Actor

ROY PRICE
Movie Producer

BRETT RATNER
Filmmaker

L.A. REID
Former Epic Records Chief

TERRY RICHARDSON
Fashion Photographer

AL FRANKEN
U.S. Senator

WES GOODMAN
Former Ohio Representative

MARK HALPERIN
Journalist

JOHN HOCKENBERRY
Former Radio Host

DUSTIN HOFFMAN
Actor

ISRAEL HOROVITZ
Playwright

CHARLIE ROSE
Journalist

GILBERT ROZON
Comedy Festival Founder

GEOFFREY RUSH
Actor

STEVEN SEAGAL
Actor

BEN AFFLECK
Actor

RUSSELL SIMMONS
Music Producer

KEVIN SPACEY
Actor

GARRISON KEILLOR
Radio Host

R. KELLY
Musician

JOHN LASSETER
Pixar and Disney Animation Chief

JAMES LEVINE
Orchestra Conductor

ROY MOORE
Senate Candidate

BILL O'REILLY
TV Host

JEFFREY TAMBOR
Actor

JAMES TOBACK
Movie Director

ADAM VENIT
Hollywood Agent

HARVEY WEINSTEIN
Movie Producer

JANN WENNER
Magazine Publisher

ED WESTWICK
Actor

MATT LAUER
TV Host

MARIO VATALI
Chef

CHRIS SAVINO
Animator, Producer, Director

DAVID BLAINE
Magician

GEORGE TAKEI
Actor

JOHN BUCCIGROSS
ESPN Host

TOM ASHBROOK
NPR Host

BLAKE FARENTHOLD
U.S. Representative

DEAN WESTLAKE
U.S. Representative

TONY MENDOZA
U.S. Senator

JOHNNY LOZZINI
TV Personality

TAVIS SMILEY
PBS TV Host

DAVID MASTERSON
Actor

MORGAN SPURLOCK
Filmmaker

OLIVER STONE
Filmmaker

BOB WEINSTEIN
Producer

LOCKHART STEELE
Vox Media Editorial Director

EDDIE BERGANZA
D.C. Comics Editor

SYLVESTER STALLONE
Actor

JOHN TRAVOLTA
Actor

TOM SIZEMORE
Actor

CHARLIE SHEEN
Actor

NICK CARTER
Singer

BENNY MEDINA
Music Manager

MATHEW WEINER
"Mad Men" Creator

CARTER OOSTERHOUSE
TV Host

GERALDO RIVERA
TV Host

MARK SCHWAHN
"One Tree Hill" Creator

RYAN SEACREST
TV Host/Radio Personality

TEDDY DAVIS
Producer

DAVID GUILLOD
Producer

GARY GODDARD
Producer

ROBERT KNEPPER
Actor

JOHN SINGLETON
Director

LARRY KING
TV Host

ANDREW KREISBERG
Executive Producer

MARK HALPERIN
Political Analyst

MEL GIBSON*
Director, Actor

BILL COSBY*
Actor

ROMAN POLANSKI*
Director

Past allegations.

CASEY AFFLECK
Actor

JOSEPH COLANERI
Metropolitan Opera Conductor

Chapter 1: Introduction

Background

This dissertation examines conflict in the area of schools systems, more specifically, in community colleges. Today's community colleges are becoming very diverse. There is an increase in the numbers of older students and women, and ethnic minorities entering these institutions (Maxwell et al., 2003, p. 25). For example, the average age of a community college student is 28. Also, 45% of students are minorities. Of that percentage, 13% are African-American and 16% are Hispanic, 6% are Asian/Pacific Islander, and 1% is Native American (American Association of Community Colleges, 2011).

In terms of gender, 58% of community college students are female and 42% are male. As for socioeconomic background, 59% of full-time community college students are employed part-time (American Association of Community Colleges, 2011). The earnings of a part-time worker are substantially lower than that of a full-time worker. From the period of December 2006 to January 2008, for instance, a part-time, civilian worker in the United States earned an average of $11.34 an hour, which is much less than what a civilian, full-time employee earned, which was $21.08 an hour (United States Department of Labor, 2008). Thus, many community college students work for low wages. Also, 59% of community college students applied for aid of any kind, including 42% applying for financial aid. For students actually receiving financial aid, 46% are receiving aid of any kind, including 21% receiving federal grants, 10% receiving loans, 13% receiving state aid, and 11% receiving institutional aid (American Association of Community Colleges, 2011).

By contrast, the demographic profile of four-year college students differs slightly from that of community college students. For example, a 2008-2009 Baccalaureate and Beyond Longitudinal Study found that 67.3% of four-year college graduates are 23 years of age. Also, 73% of these graduates are Caucasian. In addition, 57.9% of four-year college graduates are female (National Center for Educational Statistics, 2011, p. 5). Finally, only 13% of four-year college graduates worked part-time (p. 7).

Many individuals turn to community colleges because these institutions offer a low-cost, convenient route to attaining a quality education. In fact, community colleges are seen as a route to higher education because of its admissions policies and diverse student populations (Dowd, 2003, pp. 92-93). In 1996, 1250 community colleges in existed throughout the United States (Cohen & Brawer, 1996, p. xvii). By 2008, there were 1202 community colleges (Mellow & Heelan, 2008, p. xv).

Community colleges exist as a variety of schools. Some are degree-granting, two-year colleges. Other community colleges take the form of junior colleges, which allows students the opportunity to transfer to four-year colleges. Also, some community colleges exist as technical schools, where students can earn either a two-year degree or diploma in technical or vocational fields (Radcliff, 2009). Community colleges are uniquely placed between high school and college (Radcliff, 2009). In addition, community colleges are open and convenient to most people due to their relatively low cost of attendance (Radcliff, 2009).

Because of the openness of the community college, many issues impact community colleges in a distinctive way. One such issue includes whether community college students are on academic parity with their counterparts at four-year colleges.

Twenty-two years ago, Lee and Frank (1990) found that the effects of both high school behavior and community college behavior determined if the student transferred to a four-year college. Also, both authors found that females and ethnic minorities in the United States were less likely to transfer from two-year colleges to four year colleges. Also, students who were in academic tracked, high school curricula were more likely to transfer to four-year colleges than non-academic track students (Lee & Frank, 1990, pp. 183-184).

In the 21st century, external student factors still affect academic performance. For instance, Bailey et al. (2006) wanted to ascertain if community college characteristics such as ethnic composition affect graduation rates. The authors found that community colleges with high numbers of minorities have a lower number of full-time students who graduate (Bailey et al., 2006, p. 510). Also, community colleges with high numbers of part-time students have a lower graduation rate (p. 510). In addition, community colleges that spend more money on instructional needs have a higher graduation rate (p. 510).

Besides academic parity between community colleges and four-year colleges, community colleges face issues with faculty conflict and instructional quality. Academic studies from decades ago pondered these issues. For example, Darkenwald (1971) was interested in knowing if department chairpersons at medium-differentiated institutions faced more conflict in reaching decisions than those at high or low-differentiated institution (p. 408). The research also found that chairpersons at medium-differentiated colleges and institutions suffered the most conflict (p. 410). Recently, scholars sought ways to study the effects of faculty quality on graduation rates. For instance, Jacoby (2006) sought to understand if high part-time faculty rates negatively affect student graduation rates (p. 1091). Jacoby discovered that an increase in part-time faculty numbers resulted in lower student outcomes (p. 1092). Additional concerns over faculty standing at community colleges may lead to decreased satisfaction among faculty members. Kim, Twombly, and Wof-Wendel (2008) examined the differences in satisfaction rates between part-time and full-time faculty members at both community colleges and four-year colleges. Kim et al. (2008) believed that faculty autonomy was threatened by factors such as centralized management and decision-making, and planning (p. 160). These factors may adversely impact satisfaction rates. After comparing the satisfaction rates, the researchers found that the vast majority of faculty members were satisfied with their autonomy. However, four-year college faculty members reported higher satisfaction rates than their community college counterparts in regards to autonomy (Kim et al., 2008, p. 166).

Statement of the Problem

As different groups of students interact on campus, conflicts may occur due to cultural differences. For instance, a younger student may respond to a conflict differently from an older student. Likewise, male or African-American students may respond to a conflict differently from whites or females. This could be especially true if these groups do not coexist frequently. This is important because community college student involvement tends to occur within the classroom (Chang, 2005, p. 771), where conflicts between students may disrupt the educational process on campus. For example, Dee, Henkin, and Holman (2004) discussed that disagreement over the practice of religious doctrine at Catholic colleges can redefine the notions of academic freedom among faculty members (p. 179). A better understanding about how different students react and manage conflict is a key to developing conflict resolution training that can be incorporated as part of the college activities to develop conflict resolution skills among community college students.

This dissertation discussed the effects of individual demographic factors such as age, ethnicity, gender, and socioeconomic background on responses to conflict among randomly selected community college students in the United States. In addition, previous research regarding conflict in the community college setting was examined.

Goals

The first goal of the research was to provide information on how specific diversity variables impact the response to conflict situations at community colleges and how this knowledge could be used to develop conflict resolution approaches for specific groups of students. The second goal of the research was to contribute to the body of knowledge on community college students and conflict resolution, since there are few studies in this area.

Research Question

Using a Quantitative Methodology the researcher examined the following research questions and hypotheses:

Do different social and economic variables such as age, ethnicity, gender, and socioeconomic background impact students' response to instances of conflict?

Hypotheses

H1:   Students of different ages will have different responses to conflicts on community

college campuses.

H2:   Students of different ethnicities will have different responses to conflicts on

community college campuses.

H3:   Students of different genders will have different responses to conflicts on

community college campuses.

H4:   Students of different socioeconomic backgrounds will have different responses to

conflicts on community college campuses.

Definition of Conflict

Conflict can be associated with need, power, or recognition. Kreisberg (2003) defined conflict, or social conflict, as the belief of two or more people that their objectives are incompatible (Kriesberg, 2003, p. 2). Examples of incompatible objectives are incompatible positions or goals (p. 3). Kriesberg also mentioned that adversaries engage in conflicts over interests or values because those interests, such as land or oil, are believed to be limited. As such, one side may lose as one side may gain. Some resources are not material, but social, and that conflict between opposing parties may affect their power or prestige (p. 7).

In the case of community college students, individuals from different cultural backgrounds may have different needs, such as security and recognition. An individual student from one ethnic group may need recognition, for example. Another student from a different ethnic group may not understand the former's need for recognition. Thus, conflict may result.

Many types of conflicts may arise on community college campuses that may disrupt the educational process. Since the literature for community conflict on college campuses is scarce, the author used examples from four-year colleges and universities. The rationale was that many students from both types of colleges are similar in age and may face similar conflicts. One such four-year college, St. Mary's College of California, defined four types of conflict in the academic setting; Inner conflict, which involves internal tension and anxiety, conflicts between employer and employee, such as a faculty member and a dean, conflicts among faculty members, and conflicts between faculty and students (St. Mary's College, n.d.). The author believed that the aforementioned types of conflicts may also be present at the community college level.

For the purposes of the research, the author was interested in how different groups of students respond to conflicts. Among groups of students, for example, African-American students may react differently to conflict than white students due to cultural differences. Likewise, women and men may respond differently to the same conflict due to gender differences. The researcher used detailed surveys to determine the differences in responses to conflict. The researcher wanted to examine these differences in order to bring greater awareness and understanding among community college students.

Instrument: CDP

The author utilized the Conflict Dynamic Profile-Individual (CDP-I) instrument to measure conflict responses. The instrument has its roots in the Conflict Dynamic

Model. According to the Conflict Dynamic Model, conflict is complex, unraveling with time. The conflict process consists of a precipitating event that leads to conflict. Such an event may involve a difference in behavior between parties or a disagreement involving disparate needs or ideals (Capobianco, Davis, & Kraus, 2008a, p. 2).

Responses to conflict may take a constructive or destructive turn. For instance, constructive responses tend to focus on the issues of contention, rather than on the parties themselves. As such, conflicts may even get resolved (Capobianco et al., 2008a, p. 2). Conversely, destructive responses tend to focus on personal issues, which may fuel conflict beyond its origins (p. 2).

In addition to examining constructive and destructive conflict, the CDP-I measures whether conflict responses are active or passive. When someone responds actively to conflict, they are outwardly taking steps to address the issue at hand. As these steps are outwardly taken, the response itself may be constructive or destructive (Capobianco et al., 2008a, p. 3). Alternatively, a party may employ a passive approach, which takes little active effort, and in doing so, may respond in a constructive or destructive manner (p. 3).

The CDP-I recognizes all of the aforementioned behaviors and thus arranges the responses into four categories: active-constructive, passive-constructive, active-destructive, and passive-destructive (Capobianco et al., 2008a, p. 3). Examples of active-constructive conflict include perspective-taking (PT), creating solutions (CS), expressing emotions (EE), or reaching out (RO). If the individual acts passively, then he/she could exercise reflective thinking (RT), delay responding (DR), or practice adapting (AD). Responding constructively may even decelerate conflict (Capobianco et al., 2008b, p. 5).

If a party responds in an active-destructive manner, he/she may try to win at all costs (WI), display anger (DA), demean others (DO), or retaliate (RE). However, if a party responds in a destructive, passive manner, then he/she may practice avoidance (AV), yielding (YL), hiding emotions (HE), or self-criticize (SC). In short, destructive responses lead to escalating conflicts (Capobianco et al., 2008b, p. 5).

In addition, the instrument recognizes that there are certain behaviors that can precipitate a conflict. These behaviors are called hot button behaviors. Examples of hot button behaviors include displays of unreliability, overly-analytical behavior, unappreciative behavior, aloofness, micro-managing, self-centered behavior, abrasive behavior, untrustworthy behavior, and hostility (Capobianco et al., 2008a, p. 6). These behaviors give meaning to the expression "you're pushing my buttons."

The CDP-I was chosen by the author for several reasons. First, the CDP can measure a person's behavior by describing how that person feels before, during, and after a conflict. Also, the CDP allows an assessment of how the individual, as well as bosses and peers, feel before, during, and after a conflict (Capobianco et al., 2008b, p. 7). Furthermore, the CDP gives a complete conflict profile of an individual by offering feedback five aspects. First, the CDP focuses on behaviors that may provoke a reactive behavior, or hot buttons. Second, the CDP examines how the individual typically responds to conflict. Third, the CDP looks at how other people view that individual as he/she responds to conflict. Fourth, the CDP examines the Dynamic Conflict Sequence, which is defined as how individuals respond before, during, and after conflict. Fifth, the CDP measures which conflict responses can harm a person's position in the organization, which is called Organizational Perspective on Conflict (Capobianco et al., 2008b, p. 7).

The researcher was impressed with the thoroughness of the CDP, and thus selected the instrument. Also, the CDP was the culmination of two years of revision and testing. The first version was written in the spring of 1998 and was revised two more times, until a final version (the present CDP) was accepted (Capobianco et al., 2008b, pp. 9, 13).

The researcher found that the CDP has several applications. According the Capobianco et al. (2008a), the CDP can be used for conflict resolution (resolving specific conflict issues), leadership development (handling conflict effectively), career development/individual coaching (helping to move into demanding career roles), or team building (conducting team intervention to build cohesiveness) (pp. 10-11).

Conceptual Framework

Social Exchange Theory

The author will utilize the concepts of Social Exchange Theory to explain its relevance to cases of conflict between community college students of diverse cultural backgrounds. Social exchange theory may be defined in terms of understanding both exchange networks and social exchange. First, exchange networks are social ties that connect and control interactions between parties. Lawler, Thye, and Yoon (2008) state that social exchanges occur when parties give and receive valuable items (p. 520). This definition is similar to the exchange theory definition offered by Cheung and Chan (2010). Both authors stated that exchange theory referred to any action taken by a person or group results from a reward. For example, actions such as volunteering, cooperation, or marriage are committed with the expectation of some sort of compensation (Cheung & Chan, 2010, p. 210). Cheung and Chan referred to this type of exchange as reciprocity (p.

210). Reciprocity, according to the authors, is based on the principles of fairness and need for a reward (p. 210). In addition, exchange theory states that interaction alone is not enough. For example, if reciprocation is not practiced in close relationships, then those relationships are not advantageous for the parties involved (Cheung & Chan, 2010, p. 210). In social exchange theory, the act of reciprocity occurs within what Lawler et al. (2008) refer to as a micro-social order, which is the group-like social network in which social exchange takes place (p. 520). The authors explicitly defined micro-social order as a pattern of social activity such as exchange, which occurs between several parties (Lawler et al., 2008, p. 520). The extent of micro-social order is dependent on four aspects. First, involved parties exchange with members of the group. Second, global emotions are felt due to those interactions. Third, all involved people believe that they are a social unit. Fourth, each party develops attachments for the social unit (Lawler et al., 2008, p. 520). The authors also believed that as a group continues to practice exchange, emotional bonds will develop between group members and members will work collectively as a unit (p. 520).

The basic premise of social exchange theory is the maintenance of relationships among all parties as long as the benefits of the given relationship are better than in other relationships (Lawler et al., 2008, p. 520). Because of this component of social exchange theory, reward and power are associated with this theory (p. 520).

Social exchange theory contains a relational aspect that can be approached either from an individualistic or collectivist standpoint (Lawler et al., 2008, p. 522). Where the individualistic standpoint involves exchange taking place based on individual interests, the collectivist approach, by contrast, involves the consideration of the norms of a group when there is an exchange (Lawler et al., 2008, p. 522). The affect theory of social change, developed by Lawler et al. (2008) is a bridge between the individualistic and collectivist approaches. The affective theory is unique because it starts out as an individualistic assumption but demonstrates how actors develop social ties (p. 522). Lawler et al. (2008) believed that affective social exchange is different from other types of social exchange for three reasons: first, structures such as social identity processes can transform group interactions from transactional to relational; second, the transformation may lead to exchanges that take place over time; and third, the manner in which relational transformation occurs is emotional (p. 522).

Aside from affective social exchange theory, social exchange theory draws upon influences such as distributive justice. Whereas some areas of social exchange theory concentrate on deepening social relationships within the group, other areas of social exchange focus on the inequality of the exchange. Molm, Collett, and Shaefer (2006) explained the concept of distributive justice, and how it affects social exchange. According to the authors, distributive justice is defined as the evaluation of fairness of the goods being exchanged (Molm et al., 2006, p. 2332). Distributive justice may be evaluated in terms of justice expectations and social comparison. Justice expectation is an evaluation of fairness based on social expectations or experiences that a given group encountered in the past. Social comparison refers to the comparisons that a group of people may make between the rewards that they receive versus rewards received by other groups (p. 2332).

The concept of distributive justice is related to social exchange through negotiated and reciprocal exchange. According to Molm et al. (2006), negotiated exchange involves parties agreeing to benefits that can be equal or nonequal, whereas reciprocal exchange pertains to individual parties performing an act of exchange, not knowing if the act would be reciprocated (p. 2333).

In the course of the author's dissertation research, the theory of affective theory of social exchange will be used. The rationale for this decision rests in the assumption that community colleges can be considered social units made of individual students, faculty, and staff. The students who attend community colleges are exchanging their individual inputs for group outcomes. For instance, each community college student has his/her individual goals, such as transferring to a bachelor degree-granting institution, or earning an associate's degree in art. Once at the college, the student will exchange ideas with other students and will form a group with shared goals. The outcome of the exchange experience may be measured in terms of degree attainment or college transfer. In terms of conflict resolution, individual student responses to conflict can be studied using the affective social exchange theory because diverse groups of students may respond differently. It is through that response that community college students from various social backgrounds can learn to understand how each group manages conflict. Once different groups understand how conflict is managed within a given group, then there may exist ways in which these groups can better communicate their feelings and misgivings. Better communication may lead to exchange of ideas that may foster increased cooperation on campus.

Justification

As an adjunct community college instructor, the author is exposed to students from various social backgrounds, and in some cases, different countries. The author has been intrigued by diversity since childhood, primarily since the author is part Nigerian, part African-American. Also, the author lived in Africa, the Caribbean, and throughout the United States. Having been exposed to multiple cultures as a youth and as a faculty member at a community college, the author wanted to undertake a study that examined conflicts between community college students of diverse cultural backgrounds. In doing so, the author intended to conduct the study for three reasons. First, there is a cultural need for multiple social groups to interact. At the community college level, students are concentrated in a classroom for at least two hours while the instructor is imparting information. During this time, students offer their viewpoints based partly on their social background. Students learn from each other by understanding various points of view. The intent of the research project is for students to gain perspective through interaction. Second, the study of conflict resolution at community colleges is helpful to the field of dispute resolution because data from the research may be useful to community college deans faced with disciplinary infractions on campus. From the author's experience as an instructor, students who respond negatively to conflict tend to argue or fight in the classroom, the parking lot, or other places on campus. Typically, administrators holding the rank of dean of students are tasked with deciding whether the conflicting parties should be given a warning or face suspension from the college. The results of the research may be utilized as a tool for which alternative options can be employed, which may result in students resolving their issues in a constructive manner. Third, research regarding conflict resolution in community colleges is limited. Because of its limited attention, the results of the research may add to the volume of academic literature and may foster further study into the social aspects of community college students. Since many American college students are choosing community colleges as their primary source of postsecondary education, the researcher sees an increase in conflicts as more students interact with one another on a daily basis. The proposed research may equip academics with resources to address disputes on campus and to offer solutions through negotiation and mediation workshops, as well as a wellspring of dispute resolution services to student affairs and development departments at community colleges.

Chapter 2: Literature Review and Theoretical Framework

Literature Review

The literature review is divided into three relevant sections. The first section will describe a brief history and development of the community college. The second section will discuss current debates regarding the feasibility of community colleges. The third section will discuss the issues of age, ethnicity, gender, and socioeconomic background in the community college setting. Afterwards, the researcher will briefly discuss the response rates of participants in the educational setting.

Brief History of the Community College

What is a community college? The name "community college" has been used repeatedly to refer to two-year colleges. According to Arthur Cohen and Florence Brawer (1996), there are 1250 community colleges in the United States. Out of these schools, 1/6 of them are private schools. The remaining colleges are located in every state (Cohen & Brawer, 1996, p. xvii). As of 2008, there were 1202 community colleges (Mellow & Heelan, 2008, p. xv). However, two-year colleges have been called trade schools, technical colleges, or junior colleges, as well as community colleges. One may assume that there are distinct differences between these colleges, and they do indeed exist. Nonetheless, community colleges can encompass all of the above institutions. The following schools can be characterized as community colleges:

A. Two-year colleges: These institutions award a two-year degree, which is the highest degree. This type of community college offers general and liberal education, career and vocational education, and adult/continuing education (Radcliff, 2009).

B. Junior College: These colleges offer general and liberal education courses so that one can transfer to a college offering a bachelors degree (Radcliff, 2009).

C. Technical College (Technical Institute): Technical colleges offer two-year degrees and diplomas in technical, vocational, or career fields (Radcliff, 2009).

Community colleges are positioned between secondary and higher education (Radcliff, 2009). These schools are open to all who have a high school education. Community colleges also provide services to adults seeking to complete secondary school. Furthermore, community colleges attract students who live nearby and need a low-cost education (Radcliff, 2009).

Historically, the community college was first invented in the United States (Radcliff, 2009). Mellow and Heelan (2008) described community colleges as uniquely American. Community colleges educate almost one-half of American undergraduate students. In fact, community colleges educate many ethnic minorities, women, poor people, and working students (Mellow & Heelan, 2008, p. xv). The road towards the establishment of junior colleges evolved out of several movements in American history. One such movement involved community boosterism. Most American colleges were started with a charter from the King of England. The first junior colleges, however, did not seek such authority. Instead, many cities established colleges through religious denominations. The presence of colleges added to a city's cultural landscape, along with other amenities such as museums and opera houses (Radcliff, 2009). The founding of these colleges often depended on the social makeup of the community. If a town was mostly Lutheran, so was the college (Radcliff, 2009). Early proposals included schools that would provide general education to most people (Cohen & Brawer, 1996, p. 6). Proposals for junior colleges were proposed by academics such as Henry Tappan, University of Michigan's president (1851), and William Mitchell, a University of Georgia trustee (1859) (Cohen & Brawer, 1996, p. 6). The premise was that universities would be relieved of the task of teaching general courses. That way, universities can focus on research and professional development (Cohen & Brawer, 1996, p. 6). The educational programs offered by the schools varied tremendously. Also many of these colleges were poorly financed. As a result, many colleges founded in the 19th century failed (Radcliff, 2009).

By the end of the 19th century, two-year colleges underwent a dramatic shift. Because of economic downturns such as the Panic of 1893, Reverend J. M. Carroll, Baylor University president, suggested at a convention of Baptist colleges gathered from Texas and Louisiana that small Baptist colleges reduce their course load and offer two year programs. Third and fourth-year students can then finish their education at Baylor University. Reverend Carroll's vision was one of the events that led to the eventual establishment of two-year colleges (Radcliff, 2009).

Another innovator of the junior college was William Rainey Harper. As president of the University of Chicago, Harper believed that the academic standards of American liberal arts colleges were inadequate (Radcliff, 2009). Like earlier presidents such as Tappan, he also felt that colleges should discard their first two years of school. In fact, many college presidents, including Harper, agreed with the theory that the first two years of college belonged to high school (Zwerling, 1976, p. 45).

The intent of the forefathers to create community colleges stemmed in part from the desire to preserve the academic standards of the university while diverting some students to the newly developed institution (Zwerling, 1976, p. 43). Many founders were educated in German universities (p. 43). They sought to emulate the German gymnasium concept, which would be equivalent to the future junior college (p. 44). The founders wanted to remove the first two years of college from the university system so that university can focus on professions such as law or medicine. The establishment of this system would leave the university open to the intellectuals in the elite class; in turn, the university would not have to contend with secondary school courses (Zwerling, 1976, p. 44). The future junior college would be cast as a new form of high school, or gymnasium. Students who passed through this new school will be eligible for university (p. 44). Harper, for instance, believed that junior colleges affiliated with their university counterparts, would accept college credit from transferring students (Radcliff, 1986, p. 13). Thus, Harper wanted to create junior colleges as part of his overall plan to make the American system of education efficient and orderly (Radcliff, 1986, p. 14).

However, no college was willing to rebuild their institutions to suit the German model (Zwerling, 1976, p. 45). This was partly due to economic constraints and the tendency of colleges to rely on tuition from freshman and sophomore students as well as state subsidies (p. 46). Even Harper saw the futility of universities removing the first two years from their institution. Instead, Harper devised a plan to create a division within the University of Chicago that would be called the 'academic college' in 1892 (Zwerling,

1976, p. 46). The academic college consisted of the lower divisions of the departments of liberal arts, literature, science, and practical arts (Radcliff, 1986, p. 14). The upper divisions, in turn, would become the 'senior college' (p. 14). Eventually, the academic college gave way to the junior college within the University of Chicago in 1896 (Zwerling, 1976, p. 46). However, students from lower divisions took upper level classes and vice-versa (Radcliff, 1986, p. 14). Despite this, Harper extended the idea to Chicago high schools. High schools will expand their curriculum to include college courses. Students who completed college coursework in high schools would be favored for selection into the University of Chicago (Zwerling, 1976, p. 47). One such high school was Joliet High School, which became a junior college in 1902 (Zwerling, 1976, p.47).

The second junior college was founded in Fresno, California in 1910 (Dougherty, 1994, p. 115). This college was created by Alexis Lange, Dean of the School of Education at the University of California at Berkeley, and David Starr Jordan, who served as Stanford University's president (Zwerling, 1976, p. 47). However, Lange could not initially create a new college. He had to contend with the separation of California-Berkeley into an upper and lower division setting (Zwerling, 1976, p. 48). On the other hand, Jordan preferred the establishment of junior colleges. In 1910, the Fresno Board of Education passed a resolution to expand high school curriculum to include college work (p. 49). Incidentally, a 1907 legislation in California allowed for the creation of junior colleges that provided courses that would equate to the first two years of college (p. 49). Vocational education was also added to the curriculum (p. 49). Thus, the local resolution, along with the 1907 state legislation led to the founding of Fresno's first junior college.

Growth of junior colleges occurred throughout the 20th century. In 1906, there were 16 junior colleges throughout the country. Only two of those colleges were public (Radcliff, 1986, p. 14). By 1919, "39 community colleges were operating in eleven states; seven in the Midwest; three in the West; and one in the South" (Dougherty, 1994, p. 114, 118). However, many smaller colleges perished due in part to the creation of the junior college. Harper's suggestion that four-year colleges relinquish their lower divisions led to the closing of 40% of small colleges with 150 or less students by 1940. Interestingly, 15% became junior colleges (Cohen & Brawer, 1996, p. 7).

Growth continued through the 1920s. In 1922, seven states created junior colleges with 137 out of 207 colleges being privately-supported (Cohen & Brawer, 1996, p. 13). Many of these private schools were located in the South while most public schools tended to be located in the Midwest and the West (p. 13). Also, 20,000 students attended junior colleges in 1922. Most of the public schools, for instance, contained only 150 students (Cohen & Brawer, 1996, p. 13).

By 1930, the number of junior colleges increased to 450. Only five states did not possess junior colleges. There were now 70,000 community college students. California even possessed 20% of all junior colleges. In ten years, the number of junior colleges increased to 610 (Cohen & Brawer, 1996, p. 14). In 1949, junior college enrollment reached its highest point. There were 322 private two-year colleges. However, enrollment at private schools has been steadily declining. Many schools closed or merged with larger schools. Since the mid-1970s, no new private junior colleges were created. Most private junior colleges continued to have small student enrollment, even into the 1980s (Cohen & Brawer, 1996, p. 14).

Throughout the 20th century, different states developed community colleges at various stages. In the Northeast, many places lacked community colleges until recent decades. New York, for instance, did not have community colleges until the 1950s. Indiana and Maine have vocational technical institutes combined with preferred university branches. Hawaii, Kentucky, and Arizona have two-year colleges organized under the auspices of state universities. South Dakota does not even have a community college or university branch. Some states, such as Connecticut, New Mexico, Ohio, and Pennsylvania, have both community colleges and two-year university branches (Dougherty, 1994, pp. 118-119).

Two-year colleges underwent a name change, starting in the 1940s and 1950s. The term 'community college' was coined by President Truman through the Truman Commission. The name was applied to schools that served local needs (Radcliff, 2009). The Truman Commission, originally called the President's Commission on Higher Education, was formed in 1946. George F. Zook, its director, was tasked with assessing the need for higher education in a workforce affected by World War II. The Truman Commission initiated state and local funding of community colleges (Mellow & Heelan, 2008, p. 6). Throughout the 1950s and 1960s, however, some colleges continued to be called junior colleges. Junior colleges referred to lower branches of private or church-supported schools while the term 'community college' referred to larger, comprehensive public schools (Cohen & Brawer, 1996, p. 4).

By the 1980s, the growth of community colleges ceased (Dougherty, 1994, p. 118). Despite the cessation of growth, enrollment increased, mostly in larger schools. Also, the rate of growth varied according to state. For instance, at the beginning of the

1960s, California's community college system grew to "accumulate three-fifths of the community colleges it has today" (Dougherty, 1994, p. 188). Community college enrollment continues to increase to the present day. In the fall of 1991, for instance, a third of community colleges had student enrollments of between 6000 to more than 30,000. In the early 1990s, more than one million students attended community colleges with more than 20,000 students (Cohen & Brawer, 1996, p. 16).

Current Issues Affecting Community Colleges

Academic Parity of Community Colleges

Several issues impact community colleges. One such issue includes whether community college students are on academic parity with their counterparts at four-year colleges. Valerie Lee and Kenneth Frank (1990) discussed social and academic factors that facilitate the transfer of community college students to four-year colleges. According to Lee and Frank, some researchers argue that although open-door policies of two-year colleges certainly increased access to education in recent years, the increase does not necessarily mean an increase in transfer to four-year colleges (p. 178). In fact, some studies indicate that the number of transfers is very small. Citing a 1977 study by the former United States Department of Health, Education, and Welfare, Lee and Frank mentioned that community colleges enroll at least one-third of all American college students, yet less than a quarter of community college students transfer to four-year schools (Lee & Frank, 1990, p. 178). Even community college students enrolled in "academically oriented" programs are 10-20% less likely to receive bachelor's degrees than their four-year counterparts (pp. 178-179).

With respect to the study conducted by Lee and Frank, 30,000 randomly-selected high-school seniors from a 1980 High School and Beyond study were utilized in the study. These students were from 1000 randomly-selected high schools (Lee & Frank, 1990, p. 180). In addition to the original sample, a large sub-sample was also obtained from students after two years and four years of high school (1982 and 1984, respectively) and after high school graduation (p. 180). The total sample number for the first part of the study was n=10,815 (p. 180).

The authors examined the following variables, which were organized into 1) path A, which examined the effects of social background on high school academic behavior, 2) paths B and C, which examined the effects of students' academically related behaviors in high school on high school outcomes, 3) paths D, E, and F, which looked at the effects of background, high school behaviors, and high school outcomes were measured against behaviors in community college, and 4) paths G, H, I, and J, which discussed the effects of background, high school behavior, high school outcomes, and community college academic behavior on the ability to transfer to a four-year college (Lee & Frank, 1990, p. 181). The authors estimated the cumulative effects of both high school behavior and community college behaviors would determine if the student transfers to a four-year college.

The statistical method employed in the study was ordinary least squares regression, which was calculated using a program named LISREL IV (Lee & Frank, 1990, p. 181). All paths were tested using this method because ordinary least squares are used to determine path coefficients (p. 181).

The results were extensive. In the case of background, black students were slightly less likely to attend a two-year college than a four year college but were almost twice as likely to attend college rather than go to work after high school. Also, Hispanics were twice as likely to go to two-year colleges than four-year colleges and slightly more likely to go to work as students who were non-working, non-college group. Furthermore, females were more likely to go to college after high school than to go to work after high school (Lee & Frank, 1990, pp. 183-184). As for academic orientation, 39% of community college students were from the general rank and 39% were from the academic rank. However, four-year college students were twice as likely to come from the academic tracks (Lee & Frank, 1990, p. 184). As far as transferring to a four-year college was concerned, more males transferred than females. Also, blacks and Hispanics were 4% less likely to transfer to four-year colleges than whites. Furthermore, community college students who transferred were twice as likely as non-transferees in the academic track in high school. In closing, Lee and Frank demonstrated that community college students from strong academic backgrounds are more likely to transfer to a four-year college than non-transferees.

A more recent study that examined parity of community colleges examined the impact that community college characteristics have on student outcome, especially rates of graduation. Characteristics may include student body size, numbers of ethnographic minorities and women, as well as the levels of funding at each community college. Bailey et al. (2006) explored the measurement of graduation rates among community college students as part of a broader effort by educators and policy makers to measure accountability in community colleges. According to the authors, community colleges are open-door institutions that offer students access to college (Bailey et al., 2006, p. 492). However, there has been a movement towards measuring student outcome from the time they start college, leading up to graduation. This movement of accountability led to the creation of the Student Right-to-Know and Campus Security Act (1999), which amended the Higher Education Act. The act required colleges to report data on graduation rates. This data is known as Student Right-to-Know (SRK) data (Bailey et al., 2006, p. 492). Part of the reason for the need for increased accountability is the pressure that community colleges face in securing state funding, which is already difficult. As a result, community colleges increase tuition in order to meet expenses. At the same time, there is need to determine what is the most effective method of assessing student outcome (Bailey et al., 2006, p. 492).

Bailey et al. (2006) wanted to accomplish two goals in the research. The first goal was to establish a way to measure student outcome. The second goal was to find policies that can improve student outcome (p. 492). Bailey et al. described the use of assessments to measure accountability among college students. According to Bailey et al., there is no uniform method of assessment among colleges; this is unlike K-12 education, which relies upon test scores to determine student performance (p. 493). Four-year colleges use 6-year graduation data to assess accountability (p. 493). Community colleges, on the other hand, utilize the Student Right-to-Know (SRK) rate to measure community college performance. The SRK rate is a graduation rate for community college students within 150% of the time in which they would need to complete a degree (Bailey et al., 2006, p. 493). To determine the SRK rate, all incoming students are catalogued from the first day of enrollment through three years, which is 150% of the time usually needed to complete a two-year degree. The ratio of students who complete the degree in that three year period to all of the students who began taking classes at the college (p. 493). The SRK data, according to Bailey et al., is advantageous as a means of measuring student performance because the data on 1000 community colleges are available for use. Because of this, SRK data are the only source of assessments that are available for such a large number of these colleges (p. 494).

Despite the availability of SRK graduation rate data, many community college advocates object to its use to determine accountability among students for three reasons. First, graduation rates alone do not measure student outcome because not every community college student may wish to graduate. Community college students, argue advocates, have different goals. As such, measuring success by graduation rates alone may be unfair to the institution's purpose (Bailey et al., 2006, p. 494). Second, the success rate of community college students may be affected by issues that are beyond the control of the community college itself (p. 494). Third, advocates believe that the use of the SRK rate itself has limitations. For example, students who transfer to other schools in order to graduate are classified as dropouts according to the SRK rate. Thus, even students who successfully transfer and complete their education at other colleges are not considered successful by the SRK rate, which is supposed to measure outcome itself (p. 495). Because of these reasons, Bailey et al. warn that the SRK rate should be used carefully because its use may portray community colleges in a negative light (p. 495).

The authors suggested several alternatives to comparing community college outcomes other than the graduation rate alone. One method is to group the institutions by the environment, such as urban, rural, or suburban. The National Center for Educational

Statistics (NCES) is a computer program that categorizes schools by size or urban setting. Also, the National Community College Benchmark Project groups community colleges by school characteristics, as well as retention and graduation rates (Bailey et al., 2006, p. 496).

Another suggestion to improving the comparison of community college outcomes was to utilize multivariate statistics to examine graduation rates, as well as other college characteristics (Bailey et al., 2006, p. 496). In this type of analysis, the graduation rate can be analyzed by comparing the expected graduation rate to the actual graduation rate. If the expected graduation rate is lower than the actual graduation rate, then the community college would be seen as performing higher than expected (p. 496).

The authors proceeded to review empirical research regarding the relationship between the characteristics of colleges and the rates of graduation. A 1991 study by Pascarella and Terenzini (as cited in Bailey et al., 2006), indicated that colleges that cater to students with high SAT scores and high income families have a greater graduation rate. In addition to these variables, these same colleges that cater to a high number of full-time and female students have a higher rate of graduation rate. An interesting thing to note was that according to Pascarella and Terenzini (as cited in Bailey et al., 2006, p 497), undergraduate colleges that were private, small, residential, and same sex or same ethnicity have higher student outcomes. Over a decade later, Pascarella and Terenzini, in their 2005 version of "How College Affects Students: Volume 2. A Decade of Research" (as cited in Bailey et al., 2006), found that students attending private colleges with lower enrollments had a higher graduation rates. Also, African-Americans attending historically black colleges and women attending women's institutions enjoyed a small benefit over the same social groups that attended mainstream colleges (Bailey et al., 2006, p. 497).

College characteristics that led to student outcomes, such as graduation rate, were examined by Bailey et al. (2006). For instance, a 2006 study by Scott et al. (as cited in Bailey et al., 2006) examined rates of graduation for undergraduate colleges based on data derived from the College Board's American Survey of Colleges. The research indicated that private colleges and colleges with students earning high SAT scores, higher numbers of women, and more money being spent on full-time students reported higher graduation rates. However, colleges with high numbers of older students, minorities, and part-time students had a lower rate of graduation (Bailey et al., 2006, p. 499).

Another study examined how college practices can affect the outcomes of college students. A 2004 study conducted by Habley and McClanahan (as cited in Bailey et al., 2006) utilized data from 386 colleges. High-performing schools were classified as colleges in which their two and three-year graduation rates were above the median graduation rate. Conversely, low-performing schools were classified as colleges with a graduation rate below the median graduation rate. Colleges were assigned a list of 82 retention practices. The students could choose whether each practice made a major, moderate, or even a zero contribution to retention. The results indicated that successful retention practices included mathematics, reading, and writing centers, foreign language centers, and ethnic minority programs (Bailey et al., 2006, p. 499).

Bailey et al. (2006) believed that community colleges should understand that the characteristics of their school may affect student outcome. Research indicates that the typical aspects of a community college may lead to low graduation rates. However, becoming more selective in order to increase graduation rates may cause conflict with the colleges' mission or goals (Bailey et al., 2006, p. 499).

Bailey et al. (2006) conducted their own empirical study on institutional characteristics that affected student outcome. In order to sample community college students, the authors analyzed the dependent variable, the graduation rate, by using degree completion rate (p. 501). The degree completion rate, according to the authors, is the proportion of first-time full-time (FTFT) students who entered and completed community college within 150% of the normal matriculation time of two years. In other words, FTFT students were tracked for three years (Bailey et al., 2006, pp. 501-502). The data for the degree completion rate was found in the Integrated Postsecondary Education Data Systems (IPEDS), which is a census of all colleges that is performed by the National Center of Educational Statistics; the IPEDS data itself was taken from the 2002-2003 school year Graduation Rate Survey (GRS) information (Bailey et al., 2006, p. 501). Starting in the IPEDS data for 2002-2003 school year, schools must report graduation rates and include a separate section for graduation rates of females, African-Americans, and Hispanics (p. 501). Altogether, the graduation rates of all of these students are known as Student Right-to-Know data (SRK data) (p. 501).

In terms of independent variables, Bailey et al. (2006) defined social factors as institutional factors; these factors were taken from the IPEDS surveys dealing with fall enrollment, institutional characteristics, and finance (p. 503). The institutional factors included gender and ethnic minority groups, while other institutional factors included the proportion of part-time students, the percentage of part-time faculty, and tuition (p. 503). In addition, institutional characteristics such as associate degree vs. certificate granting institution and whether the school was a technical college were included as independent variables (p. 503-504).

The results indicated that community colleges with high numbers of minorities have a lower number of FTFT students who graduate (Bailey et al., 2006, p. 510). Also, colleges with high numbers of part-time students have a lower graduation rate, even among FTFT students attending that same college (p. 510). In terms of finances, the researchers found that community colleges that spend more money on instructional needs have a higher graduation rate (p. 510). When the researchers analyzed females and graduation rate, the results were contrary to previous empirical research, which often stated that colleges with more females have a higher graduation rate than men (p. 511). In fact, Bailey et al. discovered that community colleges with a large number of female students graduated at lower rates. However, the researchers believed that women graduate at high rates, but the college itself may have a lower FTFT graduation rate (p. 511). When the researchers examined part-time female students, they found a negative association between the proportion of part-time students and the percentages of female students (p. 511). The researchers admitted that they would need to conduct further research on the relationship between part-time status and the percentage of female students at community colleges. In addition, they want to select colleges in which more than 50% of the student body is women (p. 514).

Faculty Conflict in Community Colleges

Other research explores the area of faculty conflict in colleges, which greatly affects faculty satisfaction and interest in teaching. Research in faculty conflict can be traced back several decades. Earlier researchers such as Darkenwald (1971) explored the relationship between the extent of differentiation between institutions and administrative/professional conflict. The conflict, Darkenwald explained, comes from a dual academic-departmental structure in which the bureaucratic nature of the administrative structure conflicts with the professional side manifested by the departmental structure (1971, p. 407). This conflict threatens the autonomy that most departments desire. In highly-differentiated schools, which Darkenwald described as large and research-oriented, there seems to be a firm boundary between department and administration, resulting in a great deal of autonomy. By contrast, in low-differentiated schools, the boundaries are less clear, resulting in more administrative control over departmental policy. Medium-differentiated schools are faced with problems regarding administrative and departmental boundaries. The ideal model of administrative and departmental boundaries is the highly-differentiated institution (Darkenwald, 1971, p. 408).

Darkenwald's research dealt with the hypothesis that department chairpersons at medium-differentiated institutions faced more conflict in reaching decisions than those at high or low-differentiated institutions (1971, p. 408). The independent variable, differentiation, was analyzed using Scale of Institution Differentiation (SID). The dependent variables were size, quality, and research orientation. One-hundred and fifteen schools were used in the study. The results of the indices were arranged into distributions, which were then converted to Z scores (p. 409). To measure decision-making conflict between the department heads and administration, a 23 item Likert-scale form was used (p. 409). Also, the institutions were divided into five differentiation levels using stratified random sampling. In addition, 350 chairpersons from 54 colleges and universities were sampled. Those chairs were then separated into high, medium, and low differentiation groups. SID analysis was performed on the chairperson sample (p. 409).

The results indicated that chairpersons at medium-differentiated colleges and institutions suffered the most conflict (Darkenwald, 1971, p. 410). This confirmed earlier research that indicated that high and low-differentiated institutions experienced less conflict because the barriers between administration and department heads were more evident.

Recent research is pointing to the effect of faculty employment status on graduation rates among community college students. An important aspect of community college education is the quality of the faculty. Many community colleges employ part-time faculty members for half of their instructors (Jacoby, 2006, p. 1081). Jacoby (2006) wanted to ascertain if the increasing number of part-time faculty at community colleges causes a decrease in the rate of graduation among students (p. 1081). According to the author, there is very little research on the connection between part-time faculty and student persistence/ graduation; also, a significant amount of the information that exists is outdated (p. 1082). Furthermore, counseling, developmental, and advising programs are found to be critical programs at community colleges. Yet, research studies regarding effectiveness of the design of these programs are absent. At community colleges, faculties are borne the brunt of the responsibility of providing the aforementioned programs to students (p. 1082).

Jacoby proceeded to discuss research theories that examine the relevance of graduation/persistence. These studies were performed at four-year colleges and involve the theories of academic and social integration. Academic integration involves the measurement of academic success while social integration involves student interaction with faculty and activities (Jacoby, 2006, p. 1083). These theories are applicable at community colleges. However, social and academic integration are more difficult because community colleges operate as open-enrollment, commuter campuses (p. 1083). Tied to social and academic integration is the use of part-time faculty at community colleges. Jacoby, citing Benjamin (2002), believed that the overuse of part-time faculty by community colleges may negatively affect both social and academic integration (p. 1083). In addition, the New Directions in Higher Education publication stated that poor integration of part-time faculty led to reduced qualities of teaching, student advising, and cohesion of curriculum; however, the publication did not explicitly answer whether the overuse of this type of faculty led to a significant reduction in student outcomes such as graduation (as cited in Jacoby, 2006, p. 1083).

Jacoby (2006) discussed several researchers who attempted to draw a correlation between colleges using a great number of part-time faculty and student success. In a study by Harrington and Schibik (2001) (as cited in Jacoby, 2006, p. 1083), freshmen who were sampled at one Midwestern university experienced lesser student outcomes when they were taught by a large number of part-time instructors. In a 2004 study by Ehrenberg and Zhang (as cited by Jacoby, 2006, p. 1083), it was found that for every 10% increase in part-time faculty at four-year colleges, there was a 2.65% drop in the rate of graduation among students.

There are many reasons why the overutilization of part-time faculty may lead to a decrease in student outcomes. Part-time faculty members are less likely to have doctorate degrees than their full-time counterparts. Also, part-time faculty members have less office hours, less technological usages, and lower exam preparation skills (Jacoby, 2006, p. 1084). Jacoby also mentioned that student evaluations are a way of assessing part-time instructors. Previous research found that there was little variation between student evaluations of both part-time and full-time instructors. However, part-time instructors were found to give students higher grades. The reason that part-time instructors gave higher grades lies with the fact that part-time instructors are not given long-term contracts (Jacoby, 2006, p. 1084). As such, there is little, if any, job security. Since part-time employment at colleges is contingent upon student evaluations, these faculty members feel that they have to give higher grades in order to have positive student evaluations (p. 1084).

Another factor that affects the quality of part-time instructors is compensation. Compared to their full-time counterparts, part-time instructors are paid much lower. According to the 1999 National Study of Post-Secondary Faculty, full-time instructors at community colleges earned $46,636 a year. However, part-time faculty at these institutions earned just $9782 a year (Jacoby, 2006, p. 1084). In terms of instructional hours per week, full-time teachers at community colleges teach 17.2 hours, while part-time teachers teach 8.4 hours (p. 1085). In addition, part-time faculty members are not eligible for college benefit plans. Finally, the percentages of part-time faculty members at community colleges are high, with 63.9% of faculty members classified as part time, compared to 33.9% classified as full-time (p. 1085).

The conditions of part-time teachers also have an effect on student outcome. In addition to low pay and job insecurity, part-time faculty work in environments where they do not have wide access to office space, telephones, and computers. The lack of access to these facilities makes it difficult for these instructors to remain in contact with their students for the purposes of meeting and advisement (Jacoby, 2006, p. 1085). Part-time faculty may not even serve on committees that set curriculum and planning (p. 1085). Thus, the precarious position of part-time instructors may have a deleterious effect on student retention and success.

Jacoby (2006) sought to understand if high part-time faculty rates negatively affect student graduation rates (p. 1091). The research would offer greater insight into this trend than any of the previous, aforementioned studies. In this newer study, the dependent variable in the study was the student graduation rate. The graduation rate for the study was derived from IPEDS graduation rate data. IPEDS, as mentioned in the Bailey et al. (2006) study on graduation rates, stands for integrated Post-secondary Education Data System. This set of data is gathered by the National Center for Educational Statistics, or NCES (Jacoby, 2006, p.1087). IPEDS data not only contains information on graduation rates, but also on the numbers of full-time and part-time faculty, as well as student demographic data, enrollment, financial aid, and degrees (Jacoby, 2006, p. 1087). Jacoby explained that IPEDS data on institutions has its limitations such as the omission of longitudinal student data used to track student progress (p. 1087). Other limitations include missing data on socioeconomic background and student ability (p. 1087). Despite the flaws of IPEDS data, the author stated that if researchers correctly utilize this information, colleges can be measured in terms of student outcomes (p. 1087).

Jacoby (2006) utilized several institutional characteristics as independent variables. One of the independent variables, the rate of part-time faculty, is just one of a host of variables that may affect student outcome. The number of these faculty members is determined, in part, by school resources. Therefore, Jacoby did not look at the part-time faculty rate by itself (p. 1091). Other independent variables considered in the study included tuition rates, number of students on financial aid, as well as ethnicity, urbanity, school size, the number of part-time students seeking a degree, and unemployment rate (p. 1091).

Once the dependent and independent variables were established, Jacoby (2006) sampled 935 community colleges (p. 1097). The author analyzed community college graduation rates using multiple regression analysis. The graduation rate was derived from IPEDS data (p. 1089). Another statistical analysis used was ordinary least square regression analysis, which examined institutional characteristics such as the ratio of part-time faculty, ethnicity, financial aid ratio, and college size (p. 1090).

The results indicated that increasing part-time faculty numbers result in lower student outcomes (Jacoby, 2006, p. 1092). For instance, community colleges with low part-time faculty ratios have higher graduation rates than community colleges with high part-time faculty ratios (p. 1097). In addition, an increase in the percentage of part-time students led to lower graduation rates, even among first-year students. In terms of minorities, increased minority enrollments lead to a decrease in graduation rates (p. 1093). However, the author found that an increase in the number of students with financial aid has a positive effect on graduation rates (p. 1093). Furthermore, Jacoby found that as a higher rate of a state's population enrolled in community college, graduation rates increase (p. 1093). In closing, the author found that the results were consistent with findings from other researchers that state that over-reliance on part-time faculty is a result of community colleges' efforts to save money. This trend, however, leads to a negative effect on student graduation rates (p. 1097). The negative relationship between increased part-time faculty rates and student outcome may undermine the quality of education at community colleges.

Faculty Satisfaction

Recent research involving faculty members was conducted by Kim et al. (2008), which examined factors that affect faculty satisfaction at community colleges. According to the researchers, autonomy is threatened by unions (Kim et al., 2008, p. 159). Faculty unions, however, can be designed to enable greater faculty autonomy. This has been manifested in academic senates, which since the 1970s has been responsible for full-time faculty providing a great influence over curricula at the community college (Kim et al., 2008, p. 160). Despite these trends, Kim et al. (2008), quoting Levin (2006), stated that community college faculty autonomy is facing a threat through the changing of the mission statement to emphasize income generation, centralized management and decision-making, and planning (p. 160). As a consequence, faculty members are losing some of their autonomy for the sake of management and productivity of the school's workforce. According to Levin, this is a general trend. Some researchers, though, actually believe that faculty autonomy is increasing due to unionization (Kim et al., 2008, p. 160).

Past studies concerning faculty satisfaction indicated that 80% of faculty members were satisfied with their jobs, but only 66% were satisfied with their departments while lower numbers of faculty members (38%) were satisfied with their institution (Kim et al., 2008, p. 160). In addition, faculty members at four-year colleges are slightly more satisfied with students than faculty at two-year colleges. Furthermore, full-time college faculty members were generally more satisfied than their part-time counterparts.

The research was performed using a data set from the National Study of Postsecondary Education of 2004 (NSOPFP 2004) in order to determine whether full-time and part-time faculty members were satisfied with their autonomy (Kim et al., 2008, p. 160). The total sample for the study consisted of 4664 faculty members, of which 34.2% were full-time and 66.1% were part-time (p. 164). The dependent variable was the faculty's satisfaction with their instructional autonomy, while the individual faculty variables included ethnicity, gender, employment status, hours per week spent on administrative committees, hours per week spent on general student advising, and the number of office hours per week (p. 164). Other faculty variables included the number of years that they hold their jobs, whether they belong to faculty unions, or whether faculty members held a doctorate degree (pp. 164-165). Faculty satisfaction (salary fringe benefits, teaching support) and faculty perception variables were also considered. Attitudinal variables such as faculty opinions to the extent which teaching is rewarded by the school and whether part-time, women, or minority faculty members are treated fairly (p. 165).

The statistics employed in the study included ordinary least squares regression analysis. Separate sets for part-and full-time faculty members were prepared through using ordinary least squares regression analysis. The authors also used regression analysis with faculty from four-year colleges. In addition to regression analysis, *t*-tests were used (Kim et al., 2008, p. 165).

Among some of the results reported, 95% of the respondents were satisfied with their autonomy based on occupational status. In addition, part-time and full-time faculty members reported high satisfaction rates. However, community college instructors were less satisfied than their 4-year college counterparts over autonomy but were more satisfied with their overall jobs than four-year college instructors (Kim et al., 2008, p. 166).

As of 2010, community colleges are gaining attention from the President of the United States. According to CNN.com, President Barack Obama spoke at the first White House Summit on Community Colleges on October 5, 2010 (CNN.com, 2010). This summit began one day after President Obama announced the creation of programs aimed to train community college graduates for the workforce (CNN.com, 2010). The summit was hosted by Dr. Jill Biden, the wife of Vice-President Joe Biden and a full-time English instructor at a community college near the White House. Examples of community college programs given at the summit included training initiatives between community colleges and Pacific Gas and Electric, and literacy courses offered by McDonalds (CNN.com, 2010).

Age, Ethnicity, Gender, and Socioeconomic Background in the Community College Setting

Age. Since community colleges attract students from many backgrounds, it is not surprising that conflicts arise often. In this case, age, ethnicity, and gender conflicts affect the instructional and social quality of the institution. Palazesi and Bower (2006) researched the satisfaction rate of baby boomers at community colleges through site interviews. The authors state that baby boomers (those between ages 40 and 60) account for 56% of all adult learners in community colleges and universities. They also constitute 20% of all adult learners and more than 16% of the community college population (Palazesi & Bower, 2006, p. 45). Baby boomers are in college for job-related courses, personal development, or to transfer credits to four-year colleges (p. 45). As the population of younger students (ages 18-25) will level off or drop by 2011, many baby boomers will continue to take advantage of community colleges, especially after retirement. This is perhaps because baby boomers have more disposable income than their parents, a desire to continue learning, and extensive social needs (pp. 45-46).

In the study, Palazesi and Bower examine the value importance of community colleges on baby boomers, that is, how important does this generation view the community college. The value importance, according to the authors, should be related to modified self-identity, which will determine if the student would utilize the community college again (Palazesi & Bower, 2006, p. 46). This thought is consistent with market research in which core needs and desires of target groups are examined (p. 46).

In performing the research, the authors examined value importance among baby boomers as they attended a community college. Data was collected over a two year period and consisted of several college sites. Site A was a 16,000 student campus in a large city where 19% of the students are baby boomers. Site B was a 13,000 student campus where 8% of the student population was comprised of baby boomers (Palazesi & Bower, 2006, p. 48). Seventeen respondents were recruited from the two sites and given interviews. Out of that group, eight of them were interviewed again. To make a comparison, three baby boomers who were not taking classes at community colleges were interviewed. In addition, two faculty members with baby boomers in their classes were interviewed. The modal age was 48, with a mean age of 47.5 (Palazesi & Bower, 2006, p. 49). The interviews were open-ended. After the interview process, the data was then analyzed.

The results of the study indicated that many of the baby boomers were not going to community colleges to earn money because they were retired (Palazesi & Bower, 2006, p. 50). Significant findings came in the form of reinvention. Many participants found that going to community college offered a way to transition from one life to another. It allowed one to "tweak" or improve themselves as people (p. 52). Specific results indicate that the higher the value perceptions, the higher the likelihood that the person would return to community college. Thus, the person would feel a greater sense of modification or transition.

The age of an incoming student relative to completion rate is an important factor in the enrollment of older students at community colleges. In the following study, Calcagno, Crosta, Bailey, and Jenkins (2007) sought to understand the relationship between older students returning to community colleges and completion rate. According to the authors, 35% of full-time students enrolled at community colleges in the fall of 2002 were between 25 and 65 years old. Many researchers, though, believed that older adults are less likely to complete college (Calcagno et al., 2007, p. 218); however, there is little information regarding for this trend, other than the assumption that older adults may have families and jobs. Calcagno et al. (2007), citing older research by Bean and Metzner (1985, 1987), believed that older students tended to be part-time, commuter students (p. 218). The authors, furthermore, wanted to determine if older adult students at community colleges in Florida face a lower likelihood of degree completion than their younger counterparts (p. 219). The study was a longitudinal study used to examine the enrollment trends of older and younger students, which included patterns of stopping school momentarily. The authors believed that the results of the study would help policymakers devise strategies for intervention so that students can complete their studies (Calcagno et al., 2007, p. 219).

In compiling their literary review, the authors discussed the relevance of the Human Capital Theory in the decision of older adults to attend college. Becker's 1964 work (as cited in Calcagno et al., 2007), explained that the Human Capital Theory posits that people evaluate their remaining time that they have to work, as well as costs and benefits, before deciding to enroll in college. Ideally, a person enrolls in college after high school in order to make the most amount of money during their working lives. However, since adults have shorter working lives, their decision to go to college is taken seriously by analyzing costs versus benefits (Calcagno et al., 2007, p. 219).

Empirical studies regarding degree completion are fairly new and focused mostly on the rate of drop-outs among college students. However, no one examined the completion rate of older students versus younger students (Calcagno et al., 2007, p. 220). In examining drop-out rates, education researchers believed that college students who have strong high school academic backgrounds, come from higher income families, have college-educated parents, and attend school full-time face a greater chance of completing their studies (p. 220). Many students, however, do not fall into the aforementioned categories. Calcagno et al. (2007) mentioned that earlier studies such as Bean and Metzner (1985, 1987) stated that older students were more likely to be negatively affected by factors in their environment than be positively impacted by social and academic integration. However, Calcagno et al. (2007), citing Choy (2002), stated that older students are at an advantage because they are able to work, which allows them to enjoy an income (Calcagno et al., 2007, p. 220).

Calcagno et al. (2007) found that many of the studies concerning drop-out rates among older students examine obvious environmental influences such as work or family, but they fail to look at multiple factors that are, over time, dynamic. Also, the studies only examine two points along a timeline, namely the beginning of a student's academic career and the point at which he/she ends their education (Calcagno et al., 2007, p. 220). Because of these limitations, Calcagno et al. decided to utilize a discrete-time hazard model, or EHA, which is a statistical model in which data is collected at various points throughout a period of time. In the case of this study, Calcagno et al. research one outcome, which is the completion of a degree. This is referred to as single-risk discrete-time hazard model (p. 221). Thus, the aim of the study was to determine if older community college students were less likely to complete college with a degree than their younger counterparts. Unlike previous researchers, however, the authors used the EHA model to ascertain influences at different points along the students' college path that may complicate their goal of degree completion.

Calcagno et al. (2007) explained that in deciding datasets for the study, they felt that the enrollment data from the National Education Longitudinal Study (NELS), as well as the High School and Beyond (HS&B) survey were limited to high school students who enter college within a decade of finishing their secondary school experience (p. 222). The researchers then examined the Beginning Postsecondary Students (BPS) dataset because it included older students. However, transcript information was missing, so they had to rely on Florida state data, which included transcript information and offered a larger number of samples (p. 222). The researchers sampled 42,641 students enrolled at 28 Florida community colleges as first time students. The sampled students began their enrollment in the Fall Trimester of 1998-1999 and were tracked longitudinally through Spring Trimester 2004, which was 17 trimesters. This time period was known as the event period (Calcagno et al., 2007, p. 222).

In the study, the authors determined that the main independent variable was the age group of the student, followed by other factors such as socioeconomic background, test scores, ethnicity, or gender. The dependent variable was the completion rate (Calcagno et al., 2007, p. 220). In terms of the independent variables of the study, the authors collected demographic data such as age, ethnicity, gender, and college placement test scores. In addition, data concerning academic transcript information, such as full-time/part-time status, major, grades, and earned credits were collected (p. 222).

Furthermore, Calcagno et al. expanded the age range from 17-24, which is the traditional college student age range, to 17-65. In doing so, the authors divided this broad age range into two categories: The younger group, or traditional college students, consisted of 17-20 year olds, whereas the older group, or older students, consisted of students between the ages of 25-65 (p. 222). One independent variable that was missing was socioeconomic background. According to Calcagno et al., Florida does not include that category on its school datasets. In lieu of that variable, the authors substituted socioeconomic background with the number of students receiving Pell Grants, since they believed that this variable would indicate financial need (p. 223).

The results indicated several interesting findings. For instance, women, African-Americans, and Caucasians were more likely to be older students. Also, many Hispanics tended to be younger students (Calcagno et al., 2007, p. 223). Older students were more likely to receive their GED than the more traditional route, which is the high school diploma. In terms of test scores, younger students earned 87 points higher than their older counterparts in mathematics, but earned only 29 points lower in verbal skills (p. 223). The discrepancy may be the result of older students' improvement of verbal skills as they age, as well as the lack of formal exposure to mathematics after a long absence from the subject (p. 223).

The results also found that older students were more likely to have careers and families than younger students, and older students were more likely to identify themselves as part-time students (Calcagno et al., 2007, p. 223). However, unlike younger students, older students were less likely to take remedial classes (p. 224). As for financial aid, older students were more likely to be on financial aid, especially if they had lower incomes (pp. 223-224). Interestingly, older students were as likely as their younger colleagues to be well-represented in associate degree programs. However, the research found that a greater percentage of older students were enrolled in certificate programs than younger ones (p. 224).

The empirical results from the EHA model indicated the following: Women were more likely to complete their degree than African-Americans, Hispanics, and Native Americans (Calcagno et al., 2007, p. 226). Also, older students were less likely than younger students to graduate in each trimester. However, when the authors excluded math scores, older students were 1.24 times more likely to graduate than younger students. This means that older students have a lower graduation rate because of being away from mathematics for many years (p. 226). Other results indicate that spending time in remedial courses lowers the odds of graduation because those classes do not count towards a degree. Also, any increase in the duration of the degree program lessens the likelihood of graduation (p. 227). Thus, older students have a lower chance of graduation than younger students, but not because of age. When an older student has been away from using formal math skills, the student would need more practice to catch up to their younger counterparts.

Ethnicity. Age is not the only demographic issue facing community colleges. Community colleges are among the most ethnically diverse institutions in the United States. Maxwell et al. (2003) conducted a study among first-time community college students to determine course-taking patterns based on age, gender, ethnicity, and full/part-time status (p. 22). The premise for the research was that community colleges have expanded their missions from university parallel programs to full-fledged colleges.

These colleges added remedial programs, occupational curriculum, and English asa Second Language programs (p. 22). As a result, the community college has attracted a diverse student body. For example, 58% of community college students are female, while 16% of community college students are over the age of 40. Sixty-three percent of the students are less than full time. Furthermore, minority students increased 5% from 1992 to 1997 (p. 25).

The research process involved students in their first semester of community college. The target population was from the Los Angeles Community College District. Out of 136,536 students, a sample of 13,108 was chosen (Maxwell et al., 2003, p. 26). Computerized enrollment sheets were used to gather samples of students (p. 27). As mentioned earlier, students were characterized according to age, gender, ethnicity, and enrollment status. The goal was to understand the variability of enrollment patterns of community college students. Analysis was conducted by compiling lists of introductory courses; also, transcripts were utilized instead of surveys because they provide a greater degree of reliability (p. 27).

According to the results, first-time enrollees constituted between 7.3% and 24.3% of students in introductory courses (Maxwell et al., 2003, p. 29), which indicated a wide variation of students at the community college level. In addition, there were differences in the percentages of females enrolled in certain courses. Females were overwhelmingly present in child development and office administration (p. 31). In addition, there was a high concentration of Hispanics enrolled in introductory courses such as automobile technology, remedial math, and remedial English. Hispanics were less frequent takers of computer science and business courses (p. 32). Also, high percentages of first-time students in English as a Second Language courses were Caucasians, most notably from Russia and Armenia (p. 32). African-Americans were more likely to enroll in business, office administration, and computer science courses than automotive technology. Asian-Americans were most likely to enroll in computer science and Associate of Arts (A.A.) transferable math courses and less likely to enroll in administration of justice auto technology, or child care (p. 33). Overall, Maxwell's research demonstrated that a wide variety of students are enrolled in introductory courses.

Ethnicity also plays a role in transfer rates among community college students. Wassmer, Moore, and Shulock (2004) researched the effects of this phenomenon. The authors stated that community colleges fulfilled a role in transferring students to four-year colleges. However, the transfer rate has declined as community colleges offered a greater number of services. As of 2004, the date of this article, the transfer rate for the United States ranged from 20% to 25% (Wassmer et al., 2004, p. 652). Wassmer et al. emphasized that the data on measuring transfer rates are limited. It is also difficult for scholars to agree on specific causes for the decline in transfer rates. Regardless, scholars agree that declining transfer rates can interrupt the educational aspirations of students (p. 652).

Wassmer et al. continued by discussing patterns of student transfer. For instance, not only do students transfer from two-year colleges to four-year colleges, but some two-year college students transfer to other two-year schools. The authors also noted an increasing number of students from four-year schools to two-year schools (Wassmer et al., 2004, p. 652). Wassmer et al. then proceeded to highlight the difficulty of defining transfer rates. For instance, transfer rates could be defined as the number of students transferring to four-year colleges divided by potential transfer student numbers (Wassmer et al., 2004, p. 652). In addition to this basic definition, the researchers wondered if the denominator, the number of potential transfer students, should include all students that enter the institution or students who wish to transfer (p. 652). Also, past studies indicated many disparities on how the denominator, or number of potential transfer students, is defined (p. 652). In fact, some studies reported that transfer rates varied from 25% to 52%. However, Wassmer et al. was more interested in the change in transfer rates over a period of time. The authors were also interested in how transfer rates affect diverse groups of students (p. 653).

Wassmer et al. (2004) explained several social theories regarding transfer rates based on ethnicity. Bourdieu's (1973) theory of cultural capital (as cited in Wassmer et al., 2004), posited that there are several situations to which children from a specific social group are exposed, such as culture. For instance, Bourdieu believed that socially underprivileged children are less exposed to higher cultural experiences because of the lack of education within their home environment. As a result of this cultural disadvantage, children from these environments face difficulties in managing a postsecondary setting (Wassmer et al., 2004, p. 653). Another social theory, organizational habitus, was coined by McDonough (1997). According to the organizational McDonough' organizational habitus theory (as cited in Wassmer et al., 2004), beliefs held by a social group help determine their perceptions. In the case of community colleges, Wassmer et al. believes that the community college environment can lead to students harboring lesser academic zeal, which could lead to lower transfer rates (p. 653).

Another author, Cuseo (1998) (as cited in Wassmer et al., 2004), believed that higher transfer rates are correlated to college factors such as a dedicated academic curriculum, better advisement of students wanting to transfer, the utilization of more faculty members in handling transfers, and effective coordination with four-year colleges (p. 653). The demographic pattern of students most likely to transfer from two-year colleges to four-year colleges include Caucasians, males, students with higher income, and students who scored high on achievement tests in high school (p. 654). These results were reported by Grubbs (1991) (as cited in Wassmer et al., 2004). In addition, Hurst and Bradburn conducted a 2001 research study (as cited in Wassmer et al., 2004) using longitudinal data and found similar results, including the findings that younger students exhibited higher transfer rates (p. 654). According to a 1990 study by Lee and Frank (as cited in Wassmer et al., 2004), both researchers found that students with strong academic backgrounds at the two-year college level were more likely to transfer (p. 654). However, one pair of researchers, Bailey and Weininger (2002) (as cited in Wasssmer et al., 2004), found that ethnic minorities such as African-Americans and Latinos did not have a transfer rate that was much lower than those of Caucasian students. However, completion rates for bachelor's degrees were still lower among African-Americans and Latinos than among Caucasians (p. 654). Further studies by the United States Department of Education found that a challenging high school academic program helped determine if students are able to finish their bachelor's degree. As such, the results found that students from Latino or African-American backgrounds did not undergo challenging academic programs when they were in high school (p. 655).

Wassmer et al. (2004) wanted to understand if ethnicity is a factor on the rate of transfers among community college students (p. 655). The authors see disparities in transfer rates between ethnic groups as an impediment to performance in higher education. Once these patterns of transfer are identified, the authors could use the results as a means to address this issue and remove the barriers to postsecondary education performance (p. 655). To accomplish the research, Wassmer et al. utilized transfer data from first-time freshman from 108 community colleges in California. The data were derived from the California Community Colleges Chancellor's Office. The students in the study were two sets of freshmen: One group began school in 1996 and 1997 and was analyzed for three-year rate of transfer, while another group consisted of freshmen who started college in 1994 and 1995 and were analyzed for transfer rates over a six-year period (Wassmer et al., 2004, p. 656). To clarify what is meant by the transfer rate, Wassmer et al. used two definitions of transfer rate. One type of transfer rate used in the study was the inclusive transfer rate. Wassmer et al. defined inclusive transfer rate as the division of the number of transfers by the total number of first-time freshmen (FTF) (p. 656). Students who did not wish to transfer, but later changed their minds, were part of the inclusive transfer rate. Wassmer et al. also used what was called a "narrower transfer rate" definition, which was to divide the number of students who transferred over six years by the number of fellow students who either finished 12 units or enrolled in math or English classes that are transferable (pp. 656-657). This definition was more specific because it examined students who intend to transfer within the six-year period. Students who did not want to transfer were excluded from that definition (p. 657).

Wassmer et al. (2004) used several independent variables to determine the dependent variable of transfer rates (inclusive and narrower). Some of the independent variables for student cohort characteristics included percentages of females, percentage of students under 25 years old, percentages of ethnic minorities such as African-Americans, and percentage of uninformed transfer desire (p. 657). Independent variables for school characteristics included miles to the nearest California State University, academic performance (AP) index for Recent Freshmen, and the number of students (p. 657). The authors also looked at community characteristics such as the population density, unemployment rate, percentage of high school students on free or reduced meals, and percentage of high school students learning English (p. 657).

The results indicated differences based on whether inclusive or narrow transfer rates were used. When Wassmer et al. (2004) used the inclusive transfer rate model, the results showed that during a six-year period, the percentage of high school students on free and reduced lunch programs within the county of a community college had a negative impact on transfer rates. Also, urban population centers surrounding community colleges had a positive effect on transfer rates (p. 663). When the authors used the model containing the narrower inclusive rate definition, which restricted student transfers to those taking 12 units or transferable math or English courses, it was found that there are negative influences on transfer rates among increasing numbers of Latino, African-American, or female students (p. 663). That pattern was not found in the more inclusive model, which included students who may not initially wish to transfer. In other words, the study found that among students prepared to transfer, there were lower numbers of women and minorities who transferred in California's community colleges. The results of the narrower transfer rate study also indicated that there was a positive influence in transfer rates among students earning degrees in liberal arts or general studies, as well as student population size and size of the county surrounding the community college (p. 663). Wassmer et al. believed that the ethnic disparities among Latinos and African-Americans may be due to institutional bias among the 108 community colleges throughout California. The researchers suggest that policymakers need to focus on improving community colleges serving large populations of Latinos and other minorities who are underrepresented (p. 664-665).

Gender. Gender is an important aspect of community colleges. The research regarding the role of gender at these institutions is limited. The information that is available dates from the 1980s and 1990s. Even articles published in the 2000s utilized data sets from the previous decade. One such research study was published by Sax and Harper (2007), which discussed the origins of the gender gap. Although the respondents in the study were women from four-year colleges and universities, this study may be beneficial to the study of the gender gap at community colleges because the gender gap may affect all people in society.

Sax and Harper (2007) wanted to ascertain the factors that lead to differences between males and females enrolled as college students. Both authors explained that in the past, discussions regarding gender differences were centered on the 'nature vs. nurture' debate. This viewpoint was controversial because some people believed that nurture could influence nature. Sax and Harper, quoting Genova (1989), stated that it is the socialization of gender differentiation led to differences in the function of the brain between the sexes (2007, p. 670). For instance, Dr. Lawrence Summers, former president of Harvard University, courted criticism in 2005 when he suggested that females had lesser academic aptitude than men in the areas of math and science. He stated that the aptitude was a greater factor than gender socialization (p. 670). Summers' comments led to a reassessment over the role of society in creating differentiation between genders in terms of career choices and achievements (p. 670).

The argument over the roles that nurture and nature play in sex differentiation regarding achievement is still ongoing. In terms of pre-college aspirations for historically male fields such as law, the gender gap has almost disappeared (Sax & Harper, 2007, p. 670). However, researchers found that attitudes fostered before college have an effect on college achievement. For instance, a 2003 study from Whitt et al. (as cited in Sax & Harper, 2007), sampled male and female college students on cognitive outcomes. The study found that outcomes differed between the sexes. However, Whitt et al. (2003) were not able to identify which exact factors contributed to the differences. Also, Whitt et al. suggested that further study needed to be conducted on this phenomenon (as cited in Sax & Harper, 2007, pp. 670-671).

Sax and Harper proceeded to give a brief background regarding the effects of gender socialization on gender differentiation. Both authors stated that many researchers believed that the differences between genders originated in childhood. For example, researchers feel that children copy the behavior of the parent of the same sex (2007, p. 671). Other academics, however, believe that peers, not parents, are an influence on how children are socialized according to gender (p. 671). More recent research states that pre-college sex differences may be correlated to physical activity. That is, physical activity may be evident more among males than females. The participation in physical activity has been found to foster leadership skills and higher self-esteem (p. 671).

Other research found that certain pre-college events foster differences between men and women. Girls earn grades that are equal or even higher than boys prior to college. However, girls are affected by stereotypes and tracking which leads to a declination of interests towards math and science (Sax & Harvey, 2007, p. 671). A 2004 study conducted by Barnett and Rivers (as cited in Sax & Harper, 2007), mentioned that girls lose interest in math from fourth through 12th grade. In fact, the rate of disinterest in math increased from 9% to 50%. Also, there may be some differences in course-taking patterns among girls (Sax & Harper, 2007, p. 671). These results may explain why on standardized tests, boys scored higher than girls. Sax and Harper warned, though, that there is no explicit connection between course-taking patterns, test scores, and gender (p. 671). Based on the studies regarding course-taking patterns, though, females in college tended to take courses in social sciences, health sciences, and education, while their male counterparts tended to exhibit greater interest in taking math and science course (p. 672).

Further academic studies indicated that female college students experienced differences in other areas of college life. For instance, a 1987 study by Josselson (as cited in Sax & Harper, 2007) found that female college students experienced greater anxiety in establishing autonomy. Other studies by Dawson-Threat and Huba (1996) and Jacobs (1996) (as cited in Sax & Harper, 2007), found that female college students tended to major in stereotypical female fields. Furthermore, Austin (1993) and Jacobs (1996) (as cited in Sax & Harper, 2007), found differences among sexes in various outcomes such as grade point average (GPA), degree earning, and salaries (p. 672). Sax and Harper were interested in which identifiable factors accounted for the differences between the sexes. More specifically, the authors wished to ascertain at what point in college these differences occurred (p. 672). The study was designed to counteract the notion that biology and nurture play a part in the differences between the sexes, and that college events may be an influential determinant (p. 672).

Sax and Harper measured differences in gender throughout the college experience by examining three areas: academics, personality and identity, and political and social values. Datasets for the study originated from a fall 1994 longitudinal study conducted by UCLA's Higher Education Research Institute and from a spring 1998 College Student Survey (CSS) that was a follow-up to the 1994 study (2007, p. 673). Sax and Harper sampled 17,637 male and female college students at 204 college campuses (p. 673).

The authors of the study devised 19 dependent variables, which represented various pre-college and college outcomes that resulted from gender differences (Sax & Harper, 2007, p. 673). Those outcomes were divided into three areas, which were previously mentioned. For instance, outcomes in the Personality and Identity category included social activist, artist, and leader. Also, outcomes in the Political and Social Values category included political orientation, liberalism, and gender role traditionalism. Lastly, outcomes in the Academic category included competitiveness, GPA, and math ability (pp. 673-674).

The independent variables of the study were divided into pre-college and college influences on student outcomes. The pre-college independent variables included ethnicity, income of parents, education, personality, values, college expectations, academic behaviors, and non-academic behaviors. College independent variables included institutional characteristics, peer environment, college major, and experiences in college (Sax & Harper, 2007, p. 674).

Statistical analysis was conducted using ordinary least square (OLS) for both male and female students while examining the 19 dependent variables, or outcomes (Sax & Harper, 2007, p. 675). The authors found that significant differences in outcomes occurred before college in the three areas that constituted the dependent variables. For example, in the personality and identity category, females scored lower in the outcome of physical health when compared to males. However, in the political and social values category, women scored higher in the outcome of strengthening of religious beliefs, political liberalism, and promoting racial equality (Sax & Harper, 2007, p. 677). The results from pre-college variables indicated that women were rated lower on emotional health and physical exercise (p. 679). Other pre-college variables in the study found that women tended to be more politically liberal than their male counterparts. Sax and Harper explained that the reason for the result may be attributed to lower female scoring on the pre-college variable of competitiveness. Competitiveness, according to the authors, tended to be a characteristic of persons who were politically conservative (p. 679).

Other pre-college variables pointed to differences between genders, but did not explain the gender gap. In terms of the pre-college variable of social activism (political and social values), the results found that females scored higher than males. Social activism includes activities such as volunteering (Sax & Harper, 2007, p. 680). In fact, both authors suggested that women who volunteered in high school were likely to become involved in social activism after four years of college (p. 680). When the authors measured college characteristics of social activism and compared it to gender, there were no significant differences between genders (p. 680).

Sax and Harper reported interesting findings in the academic area. Women in college who scored higher than male college students did so because they earned higher grades in high school (2007, p. 683). This is interesting because the study also found that men enter college with higher SAT scores (p. 686). The reason for higher college grades among female college students was due, in part, to greater emotional support from family members. Ironically, females were found to feel more overwhelmed in college than men. However, this stressor enabled them to earn high grades (p. 686). Sax and Harper concluded their study by stating that although some gender differences exist between male and female college students, the differences were due to pre-college influences. Also, these findings did not fully explain the gender gap between men and women (p. 686).

Another interesting article addressed the differences between genders in terms of wage differences after attending community colleges. In an article by Gill and Leigh (2000), the gender wage gap was discussed. The authors explained that the wage gap between males and females has been narrowing in the 1980s due to an increased exposure of females to the labor market and post-secondary education (Gill & Leigh, 2000, p. 163). One reason, which some research ignores, is the increase of female community college enrollment over the last 25 years. The hypothesis of the study posits that the disaggregation of secondary education into community college and 4-year college sections and shift of attention in study fields may account for the decline of the wage gap between men and women (p. 164).

In order to test the hypothesis, the authors used post-secondary data from the National Longitudinal Survey of Youth (NLSY). This data was taken from 1985-90 and 1989-94 (Gill & Leigh, 2000, p. 164). Another set of data used was the NLS72, which detailed college majors (p. 166). Sample size ranged from 2410 respondents from the 1985 sample to 3243 respondents from the 1993 sample (p. 167). According to some of the results, the wage gap for 25-28 year olds fell 0.0469 log points from 1985 to 1990. For workers 29-32 years of age, the wage gap narrowed even more by 0.0932 (p. 167). Overall, community college can be a means by which women acquire more education, thus leading to longer work experience and a chance to close the wage gap with men.

Socioeconomic Background. Students from many socioeconomic backgrounds are attending community colleges. As mentioned earlier, many students attend community colleges due to their low costs relative to other types of post-secondary education. However, many students struggle to complete their community college education based on availability of financial aid. A study by Dowd and Coury (2006) highlighted these difficulties. The researchers, citing work from Dynaski (2002b) found that low-income community college students are more sensitive to changes in college prices than relatively affluent, four-year private college students. Also, low-income community college students are more negatively impacted by debt from federally-subsidized student loans ((Dowd & Coury, 2006, p. 36). The researchers wanted to know if loans affected student outcome. To accomplish this, the study utilized survey data from National Center for Educational Statistics (NCES). These surveys were National Postsecondary Student Aid Study (NPSAS) and a follow-up survey, Beginning

Postsecondary Students (BPS), conducted from 1990/1994. Additional data was gathered from the BPS survey conducted in 1996 and 1998 (Dowd & Coury, 2006, p. 40).

Students included in the sample were those who first began classes in the first semester. Four-year college students were not included. Also, there was missing data from students who were not likely to continue their education (Dowd & Coury, 2006, p. 41). The focus on analysis was on the effect of financial aid on student persistence and graduation within five years of the study (p. 41). Negative effects may be due to high tuition rates, while positive effects may be due to financial supplements such as grants and work study programs (p. 41). Variables included financial status, financial aid package, parental status, and work hours (p. 44). Demographic variables included age, ethnicity, gender, marital and parental status, household income, and financial dependency status (p. 45).

Based on the demographic and financial results, dependent students who used loans showed a higher persistence than dependent students without loans; also, low-income students with loans were found to have a low degree attainment (Dowd & Coury, 2006, p. 50). Dowd and Coury reasoned that low-income students who took out loans were very concerned about loan default. That fear is coupled with the realization that low-income community college students earned a mean income of $29,000 (in 1990 dollars). Also, independent students with higher incomes experienced more positive effects because loan amounts were higher (Dowd & Coury, 2006, p. 54). Thus, there was a negative association between loan attainment and degree attainment for low-income students.

Dowd (2003) authored another article on the effects of socioeconomic background on community colleges. In the article, "From Access to Outcome Equity: Revitalizing the Democratic Mission of the Community College," Dowd explained the role that community colleges play in providing equal access to education for poor and minority students. Dowd refers to this role as a democratizing role, which leads to diversity and open admission policies (2003, p. 93). However, Dowd pointed out that critics believe that community colleges tend to shield four-year colleges from new students seeking a baccalaureate degree (p. 93). Also, the author believed that state governments pressure community colleges to act as efficient as businesses, preparing graduates for the business sector; in the process, tuition has increased, limiting the democratizing process for low-income students (Dowd, 2003, p. 93).

Dowd then discussed some of the roots of democratization in the community college, including the goals of President Truman's Commission on Higher Education, which was to provide equal, open access to higher education (Dowd, 2003, p. 94). As the number of community colleges increased, a comprehensive mission started to develop in which community colleges provided four components. Those components included vocational education, general education, community outreach for noncredit hours, and preparation for student transfer to four-year academic institutions (p. 95). At first, community colleges focused on transfer to four-year institutions, but by the mid-1980s, vocational training began to gain greater importance. Dowd explained that as of 2003, three-fifths of community college students are majoring in vocational programs (2003, p. 95).

Dowd mentioned that community colleges experienced a shift in mission in the 1980s. The author argued that community colleges were becoming more capitalist in that the institution is now seen as more of a training school for a labor force, than a route for transfer to four-year colleges. The growing capitalistic mission, asserts Dowd, is leading to the privatization of community colleges, which the author sees as a threat to democratization of community colleges (Dowd, 2003, p. 95). Another threat that Dowd is concerned about is the increasing differentiation of education and entrepreneurial, which is seen by Dowd as a threat to the open-admissions goals of community colleges (p. 95).

As community colleges become more selective, the tuition has also increased. Dowd argued that as of 2001, the tuition and fees of community colleges was $1705, which was double the tuition in 1968 dollars (2003, p. 103). As of 2002, the total cost of community college education, which would include tuition and fees, as well as transportation and other expenses, was $9100 (Dowd, 2003, p. 104) As a result of increased tuition; community college education has become less affordable to the poor. This is because tuition rates have increased, while the salaries of lower-income people have decreased (p. 104). Community colleges are affordable when students use loans. Citing a 2002 Federal Advising Committee on Student Financial Assistance study, Dowd explained that 52% of low-income students with high unmet need, who are academically qualified, are enrolled in community college, compared to 83% of students with low unmet need (pp. 105-106).

At the conclusion of the article, Dowd stated that although community colleges are thought of as a democratic system in which access is granted to all students, access does not always equal outcome because of increasing tuition and stratification of educational programs, which lead to inequality in outcomes among different groups of people (2003, p. 116).

Recent studies have demonstrated the relationship between education and income. Haveman and Smeeding (2006) discussed the discrepancies in education between low and high income students. For instance, 85% of eighth-graders want to go to college. However, only 44% of low-income students are able to enroll in college, compared to 80% of upper-class students (Haveman & Smeeding, 2006, p. 126). Also, a large number of low-income students tend to be concentrated in two-year colleges (p. 126). The authors then explained the significance of education as a means of upward social mobility. In doing so, Haveman and Smeeding cite John Goldthorpe's theory of an 'education-based meritocracy' (2006, p. 127). According to Goldthorpe's work (as cited in Haveman & Smeeding, 2006), a postsecondary education prevents children from inheriting their parents' economic situation (p. 127). In other words, children of poor people need not be poor themselves. Goldthorpe believed that the movement towards a society that is not as class-oriented requires three things: the relationship between a person's socioeconomic background and education should reflect their ability, the relationship between education and employment should reflect qualifications, and the relationship between education and employment must cross socioeconomic backgrounds (as cited in Haveman & Smeeding, 2006, p. 127).

Haveman and Smeeding argued that despite the goals of a meritocracy based on education, disparities in education according to socioeconomic background still occur. For instance, both authors point out that children of wealthy parents invest a significant amount of influence, money, and time on their children to make sure that they are successful from preschool through graduate school (2006, p. 128). It is because of greater affluence that these children have greater choices when it comes to selecting a college to attend. Lower-income children, on the other hand, are left with fewer choices. Although some low-income students succeed due to luck and persistence, many face obstacles to academic success (p. 128). Therefore, both authors suggested that a greater effort must be made in order to ensure that low-income students have greater opportunities to enter college by starting at the kindergarten level (p. 128).

In the study, Haveman and Smeeding sought to determine what policies can be utilized to eliminate disparities in education and income. To accomplish that, the authors examined factors that contribute to disparity, such as poverty and inadequate academic preparation of schools in low-income areas. For example, Haveman and Smeeding found that half of low-income students surveyed in their 1992 study met the minimum qualifications to enroll in college (2006, p. 136). The authors believed that schools that enroll large numbers of low-income students emphasize access over preparation. For instance, many low-income students are affected not only by poor schools, but by their families and neighborhoods. The authors, citing a similar study by Thomas Kane, also believed that low-income students were ill-prepared to take the SAT and were ill-informed about the cost of tuition and expenses (Haveman & Smeeding, 2006, p. 136).

Haveman and Smeeding suggested several avenues for improving the disparities between socioeconomic groups when it comes to academic achievement. Both authors suggest strengthening the relationship between K-12 and college through middle schools better preparing children for college (2006, p. 141). Also, colleges should not provide unprofitable services such as remedial courses, which Haveman and Smeeding suggested could be handled by community colleges (p. 141). Instead, colleges should partner with public and private agencies that can provide the aforementioned services, while providing a quality education to students; another suggestion included capping subsidies to wealthy colleges and redistributing those subsidies to less wealthy colleges (pp. 141-142).

Respondents' Attitudes towards Conflict

Research involving respondents' feelings towards a particular conflict is relevant to conflict resolution because every person's opinion is important. Several scholars use questionnaires in order to determine the extent of attitudes towards a conflict situation. Davidson and Wood (2004) studied a conflict resolution model aimed at resolving conflicts among schoolchildren in Australia. The model, named CRM-A (or Conflict Resolution Model-Australia), is comprised of four stages: to develop expectations for win-win solutions, to define party's interests, to brainstorm solutions that are creative, and to combine options into win-win solutions (Davidson & Wood, 2004, p. 7). The first stage, which is to develop expectations for win-win solutions, involves getting both parties to reframe the conflict resolution process into one that offers mutually-acceptable conclusions. The second stage, which is to define interests, emphasizes avoiding positions and focuses on underlying needs or interests. The third stage, or brainstorming, involves thinking of creative options that can benefit all sides in a conflict. The fourth stage, or combining options, involves combining ideas into strategies that can meet the interests of all sides (Davidson & Wood, 2004, p. 7).

The researchers then discussed how psychologists at the University of Tasmania, Australia, researched the CRM-A model in four studies: three involving college students and one involving high school students. In all experiments, some participants were trained on conflict resolution skills while others were not (Davidson & Wood, 2004, p. 9). Afterwards, both trained and untrained students were tested. In the testing phase, trained participants were paired with untrained participants. Before the test phase began, the participants answered a questionnaire that asked their views on social interests, such as required student union fees and smoking in public places. Also, the participants were paired based on opposite views on one of the topics. The participants were then asked to discuss the viewpoints and make recommendations on handling the issues. With the consent of the participants, the exercise was recorded. The participants in the study did not know who received training. Also, each person was rated on their communication skills and their success at reaching a win-win solution (Davidson & Wood, 2004, p. 9).

Two studies of interest are the first and second studies. In the first study, 48 participants were randomly allocated to a trained or untrained condition. The training was three hours long and was held for three weeks. During the test phase, the participants were divided into six pairs with both participants trained, along with 12 pairs with one trained and one untrained persons, and six pairs of untrained persons (Davidson & Wood, 2004, p. 9). The results of that study concluded that trained participants demonstrated higher skill levels than untrained participants (p. 9). The second experiment sought to determine how to separate effects of training in cooperation and problem-solving. In the study, 40 participants were randomly selected for training or non-training. The training sessions lasted one hour. Forty participants from the first study were assigned as untrained participants during the testing phase. The discussions were recorded and scored. The results demonstrated that skills can improve after cooperation training, especially in the area of developing win-win solutions and brainstorming (Davidson & Wood, 2004, p. 10).

Diversity and Conflict Theories

Research involving community college diversity may examine the age, ethnicity, gender, and socioeconomic background of students at a given campus. If one looks in terms of ethnicity, for example, very little research has been conducted at the community college level. According to Maxwell and Shammas (2007), there is almost an absence of research material on community college ethnic diversity, despite cultural shifts in North America (p. 344). Overall, the number of ethnic minorities in college has doubled from 15.7% in 1976 to 30.3% in 1996. This number is expected to increase over the next quarter century. However, much of the research concerning ethnic diversity is limited to four-year colleges and universities (Maxwell & Shammas, 2007, p. 344).

Despite the lack of research involving ethnicity and diversity at the community college level, several social theories that were examined at four-year colleges and universities may be used at community colleges. For instance, Maxwell and Shammas were able to explain that prejudice can be reduced through application of Allport's Contact Theory (2007, p. 345). Allport's 1954 research (as cited in Maxwell & Shammas, 2007) described Contact Theory as a belief in which contact between different groups of college students would lessen prejudice (pp. 345-346). The lessening of prejudice is contingent upon four factors such as equal group status in collegiate settings, goals that are common to each person, cooperation's among the groups, and the support of the legal or customary system (p. 346).

To summarize, Contact Theory assumes that ethnic equality, based on communication and common values may reduce prejudice on college campuses (Maxwell & Shammas, 2007, p. 346). The contact theory has been applied extensively on four-year college campus, but not on community college campuses (p. 346).

Apart from the Contact Theory, two specific conflict theories are worth mentioning. Both the Integrated Threat Theory and Social Dominance Theory explain much of the causes of prejudice towards certain social groups. As in the case of the Contact Theory, both the Integrated Threat Theory and Social Dominance Theory have been tested primarily on four-year college campuses, not on community college campuses. Despite the lack of data explaining the effectiveness of these theories, researchers such as Maxwell and Shammas (2007) mentioned that the conflict theories can be tested at community colleges, especially in the classroom, where different social groups interact most often (p. 348). For example, researching social theories at the community college level may be used to explain why there is a great deal of variation concerning enrollment by ethnicity. This may help determine the number students in remedial and college level courses based on ethnicity (pp. 347-348).

Integrated Threat Theory states that prejudice towards a particular group of people are dependent on four factors; realistic threats, symbolic threats, intergroup anxiety, and negative stereotypes (Corenblum & Stephan, 2001, p. 252). Realistic threats are defined as economic or political threats to the in-group (p. 252).

This fear may manifest itself in the expression of fear towards the out-group. Symbolic threats are seen as possible threats to an in-group's values and cultural norms (Corenblum & Stephan, 2001, p. 253). These threats manifest themselves in philosophical differences between the in-group and the out-group (p. 253). An example would be the differences in attitudes towards illegal immigration. The in-group may feel that illegal immigrants threaten the values of the dominant society, whereas some immigrants believe that illegal immigrants are just trying to seek freedom and economic stability.

Intergroup anxiety is another aspect of the Integrated Threat Theory. This aspect deals with the levels of uncomfortable feelings that develop as people from different groups interact (Corenblum & Stephan, 2001, p. 253). Some out-group members may feel social rejection from members of the in-group because of fears of embarrassment and ridicule exhibited by the out-group members (p. 253). Corenblum and Stephan argue that the out-group feels more anxiety than the in-group because the in-group is seen as more dominant in a given society. As such, whatever actions are taken by the out-group may result in consequences from the in-group; if an out-group member commits an action that is negative, then the in-group will hold them accountable for that one action (Corenblum & Stephan, 2001, p.253).

Tied to this anxiety is the existence of negative stereotypes. Negative stereotypes reflect the level of prejudice held by members of the in-group towards the out-group. For instance, some in-group members may devise stereotypes to prove that the out-group is hostile or unclean, which further fuels resentment towards the out-group (Corenblum & Stephan, 2001, p. 253). Corenblum and Stephan gave examples of high anxiety between African-Americans and Caucasian-Americans as well as other ethnic groups (p. 253).

The social dominance theory states that society is hierarchal, in which there is at least one dominant social group and one subordinate group (Seelman & Walls, 2010, p.

106). The theory examines why human beings group themselves according to hierarchy and why, for instance, there is ethnocentrism, classism, or sexism (Sidanius, Pratto, van Laar, & Levin, 2004, p. 847). Social Dominance Theory does not simply explain why certain extreme acts of prejudice occur, but focuses on subtle acts of discrimination (Sidanius et al., 2004, p. 847).

Social Dominance Theory examines all cultural and social aspects of a given society without generalization of discrimination. The theory seeks to understand the intertwining of different groups, while describing similarities and differences between the groups (Sidanius et al., 2004, p. 847). As such, Social Dominance Theory does not focus on a single cause of discrimination (p. 847). Another important aspect of Social Dominance Theory is that it explains how institutions may discriminate towards certain groups. For instance, some groups may distribute valued commodities such as food or prestige to certain groups. At the same time, social institutions may distribute unpleasant commodities such as imprisonment and death towards groups that may be seen as less privileged (Sidanius et al., 2004, p. 847). Furthermore, discrimination towards a certain group is systematic, because it is rationalized within the social institutions as ideologies (p. 847). Thus, one group may feel justified in discriminating against another group (p. 848).

Social Dominance Theory can be studied by measuring the Social Dominance Orientation. This scale measures the group's desire for dominance (Sidanius et al., 2004, p. 847). For instance, there is a correlation between the levels of social dominance orientation (SDO) and levels of prejudice towards subordinate groups (Seelman & Walls, 2010, p. 106). In other words, the higher the level of prejudice exhibited by the dominant group, the higher the levels of SDO. According to Seelman and Walls, some groups may feel justified in displaying prejudice because it can serve as a justification of their dominance (2010, p. 106).

In closing, both the Integrated Threat and Social Dominance theories posit that conflicts result between those entities who are attempting to acquire resources and those entities who are attempting to retain resources (Maxwell & Shammas, 2007, p. 347). In addition, research at the community college level is limited, so further social research involving these conflict theories may be beneficial to understanding cultural conflict based on age, ethnicity, gender, and socioeconomic background. In turn, greater understanding of conflict may lead to increased cooperation among individuals from diverse social groups.

Chapter 3: Methodology

Introduction

The type of methodology that the author utilized for the research was quantitative. Quantitative was chosen because, according to Creswell (1998), citing Ragin (1987), quantitative research examines a few variables but many cases (p. 15). If the researcher were to utilize qualitative research, then there would need to be a commitment of many field hours, followed by gathering enormous data, only to reduce the data to a few select categories. In addition, the researcher would need to write long entries involving quotes and passages incorporating different points of view. Finally, qualitative research involves the participation in research that does not have a specific guideline (Creswell, 1998, p.17).

The research required a limited number of independent variables, which included age, ethnicity, gender, and socioeconomic background. The researcher wanted to know if those variables influenced the dependent variable, namely responses to conflict. As such, the researcher believed that quantitative methodology was a better choice than qualitative methodology because of the fact that a limited number of independent variables needed to be measured for their relationship to the dependent variable. Also, the researcher dealt with a limited time schedule, in which qualitative research would be unsuccessful. Furthermore, quantitative measurements offered better accuracy in terms of interpreting variables for future use and repetitive experimentation.

Community college research used quantitative research to explore relationships between social factors of students and specific outcomes, such as graduation rates or satisfaction rates. The author gave examples of cases in which independent variables, such as age, ethnicity, gender, and socioeconomic background, as well as the dependent variable, responses to conflicts, were studied using quantitative methods.

When understanding the link between age and college satisfaction, Palazesi and Bower (2006) conducted interviews with older students, referred to in their research as baby boomers. The researchers used statistics to determine that most baby boomers went back to college to reinvent themselves (Palazesi & Bower, 2006, p. 52). Quantitative methodology was also used to understand the roles that ethnicity played in the academic outcomes of community college students. For instance, Maxwell et al. (2003) used statistics to understand if differences in ethnicity determined course-taking patterns among first-time community college students. The authors used enrollment rosters and transcripts instead of surveys because the documents provided a greater amount of information pertinent to examining course-taking patterns than surveys (Maxwell et al., 2003, p. 27). The results indicated that course-taking patterns correlated with social factors such as ethnicity. For instance, Maxwell et al. (2003) explained that Hispanics enrolled in computer science and business courses than other ethnic groups. Also, high numbers of Caucasian students from Eastern Europe took English as a Second Language courses (p. 32).

In studies regarding gender, Sax and Harper (2007) wanted to ascertain if the gender gap between males and females affected female academic performance in college. More specifically, the authors examined the possible origins of the gender gap and discovered it to begin in childhood with mimicking of the same-gender parent, and continuing through high school (Sax & Harper, 2007, p. 671). The authors used ordinary least squares to determine at which point before and during college would academic performance be affected by the gender gap. The authors found that females scored lower in personality and identity and emotional health than their male counterparts, yet higher in political and social values category than males (Sax & Harper, 2007, p. 677). However, females scored lower on emotional health and physical exercise than males (p. 679). Due to the use of quantitative research, the authors were able to ascertain several aspects to the gender gap that may be due to upbringing.

Socioeconomic background, yet another independent variable, was examined using quantitative methods. In Dowd and Coury (2006) wanted to know if loans affected student outcome. The researchers utilized survey data from National Center for Educational Statistics (NCES) (Dowd & Coury, 2006, p. 40). Students included in the sample were those who first began classes in the first semester. Four-year college students were not included. Also, there was missing data from students who were not likely to continue their education (p. 41). Variables such as financial status, financial aid package, parental status, and work hours were used (p. 44). The researchers also examined demographic variables included age, ethnicity, gender, marital and parental status, household income, and financial dependency status (p. 45). Based on the results, dependent students who used loans were more likely to stay in school than dependent students without loans (Dowd & Coury, 2006, p. 50). Also, low-income students with loans were found to have a low degree attainment (p. 50).

Quantitative data was used on in previous research involving the dependent variable of responses to conflict. For instance, Davidson and Wood (2004) utilized a conflict resolution model aimed at resolving conflicts among schoolchildren in Australia. The model, named CRM-A (or Conflict Resolution Model-Australia), is comprised of four stages: to develop expectations for win-win solutions, to define party's interests, to brainstorm solutions that are creative, and to combine options into win-win solutions (Davidson & Wood, 2004, p. 7). Davidson and Wood used questionnaires and the CRM-A model to test to determine if conflict resolution training better equips students with the skills needed to resolve conflicts. In the study, Davidson and Wood divided the students into two groups: participants who were trained on conflict resolution skills, and participants who were not trained (p. 9). Afterwards, both trained and untrained students were tested. In the testing phase, trained participants were paired with untrained participants. Before the test phase began, the participants answered a questionnaire that asked their views on social interests, such as required student union fees and smoking in public places. Also, the participants were paired based on opposite views on one of the topics. The participants were then asked to discuss the viewpoints and make recommendations on handling the issues (Davidson & Wood, 2004, p. 9). The participants in the study did not know who received training. Also, each person was rated on their communication skills and their success at reaching a win-win solution (p. 9). The results demonstrated that students' conflict resolution skills can improve after cooperation training, especially in the area of developing win-win solutions and brainstorming (p. 10).

In closing, quantitative studies provide repositories of data and results that are useful information for future scholars. The author intends to add to the body of knowledge regarding community college conflict by providing data on responses to conflict based on social background. It is the hope of the author that future scholars could use this information to further expand the understanding of this phenomenon.

Research Question

Do different social and economic variables such as age, ethnicity, gender, and socioeconomic background impact students' response to instances of conflict?

Hypotheses

H1:   Students of different ages will have different responses to conflicts on community college campuses.

H2:   Students of different ethnicities will have different responses to conflicts on community college campuses.

H3:   Students of different genders will have different responses to conflicts on community college campuses.

H4:   Students of different socioeconomic backgrounds will have different responses to conflicts on community college campuses.

Define and Operationalize Concepts and Variables

Independent Variables

Age. For the purposes of the study, age was defined as a chronological entity that ranges from 18 to 85 years. 'Years' was the unit given for age.

Ethnicity. This variable was defined as an ethnic group. In the case of the African-American category, the name "African-American" is commonly interchangeably with "Black" among non-academics. However, the use of these two terms may be confusing because many people of the African diaspora, as well as African-Americans, are often categorized as Black by many people. For the purposes of this research, the author characterized only those individuals, born in the United States of African ancestry, as African-American. Other persons of African descent born outside of the United States are not African-American, and may chose another ethnic group of their choice. Also, the word 'Black' was not used as an ethnic reference for any people in this study.

Responses were listed as E1, African-American, E2, European-American (Non-Hispanic), E3, Hispanic, E4, Asian/Pacific Islander, E5, Alaskan Native/Native-American, E6, Two or more ethnicities, and E7, Other ethnicity.

Gender. This variable was defined as a state of sexual identity. Responses were listed as male (G1), female (G2), or other (G3).

Socioeconomic background. This variable was defined as a socioeconomic class that one belonged to. To differentiate between the classes, the income level of the respondent's families was used. The responses were listed in the following manner: S1, which was up to $9,999 a year, S2, which ranged from $10,000 to $19,999 a year, S3, which ranged from $20,000 to $29,999 a year, S4, which ranged from $30,000 to $39,999 a year, S5, which ranged from $40,000 to $49,999 a year, S6, which ranged from $50,000 to $59,999 a year, and S7, which was $60,000 a year and above.

Dependent Variable

The dependent variable was the individual student's response to conflict. Student conflict was defined as the incompatibility of needs between people with incompatible goals, interests, or principles (Capobianco et al., 2008b, p. 2). Examples of student conflicts included verbal arguments, physical altercations, nonverbal gestures, and gossip. Student responses to conflict were defined as emotional responses to behavior that may lead to interpersonal conflict. Examples of emotional responses to conflict include perspective taking, adapting, or displaying anger. Responses were rated in terms of intensity through a Likert Scale. For example, the response to a question regarding response to conflict fell within the following range: A) The situation does not upset me at all, B) The situation upsets me to a small degree, C) The situation upsets me to a moderate degree, D) The situation upsets me to a considerable degree, or E) The situation makes me extremely upset. The responses generated in this manner may determine how each social group reacts to individual instances of conflict.

Instrument: The Conflict Dynamic Profile-Individual

Definition. The author utilized the Conflict Dynamic Profile-Individual (CDP-I) instrument to measure the response to conflict that may occur among community college students of various social backgrounds. The CDP-I is based on the Conflict Dynamic Model, which views conflict as complex and that conflict unfolds over a period of time. Events that occur in the conflict process consist of a precipitating event, which sets the stage for a conflict to unfold (Capobianco et al., 2008a, p. 2). The event in question may be any behavior or issue between one person and the other person. The event may also consist of anything that results in opposing interests, goals, needs, or beliefs (Capobianco et al., 2008a, p. 2).

The Dynamic Conflict Model is used to measure the time during which a precipitating event leads to the initiation of the conflict. Responses to conflict may either be constructive or destructive. Constructive responses tend to result in conflicts not becoming escalated. In fact, constructive responses may reduce tension and allow the conflict to be focused on ideas, not the personalities of the parties (Capobianco et al., 2008a, p. 2). However, some responses to conflict are destructive. Destructive responses may make the conflict worse by focusing on personalities (Capobianco et al., 2008a, p. 2).

Conflict responses are not only understood in terms of constructive or destructive, but as active or passive. Active responses involve individuals taking outward actions in response to a conflict. These responses may either be constructive or destructive (Capobianco et al., 2008a, p. 3). On the other hand, passive responses require little effort on the part of the individual. Passive responses, like active responses, may be either constructive or destructive (Capobianco et al., 2008a, p. 3).

To simplify the Dynamic Conflict Model, one can look at an individual who is at the crossroads of two choices once faced with a hot-button behavior which initiated a conflict. The individual has two choices: act in a constructive or in a destructive manner. If one chooses to act in a constructive manner, the person may act either passively or actively. Of the individual acts actively, then he/she has four choices; perspective-taking (PT), creating solutions (CS), expressing emotions (EE), or reaching out (RO). If the individual acts passively, then he/she could exercise reflective thinking (RT), delay responding (DR), or practice adapting (AD). Responding constructively could lead to task-focused conflict that consists of focusing on the task at hand and solving problems, which can lead to positive effects. As a result, tension decreases and group functioning improves. The end result is a de-escalation in conflict (Capobianco et al., 2008b, p. 5).

What if the individual chooses the destructive route? If he/she does so, then the individual may respond actively by winning at all costs (WI), displaying anger (DA), demeaning others (DO), or retaliating (RE). If the individual responds in a destructive, passive manner, then he/she may practice avoiding (AV), yielding (YL), hiding emotions (HE), or self-criticize (SC). If that individual chooses a destructive response, then the conflict becomes focused on the personality, which can lead to negative effects. As a result, tension increases, and group function is derailed. The end result is an escalation in conflict (Capobianco et al., 2008b, p. 5).

A summary of the aforementioned behavioral responses was compiled into Figure 1, which was derived from Figure 1, The Conflict Dynamic Model, in Capobianco et al. (2008b, p. 5).

<table>
<tr><td colspan="2" align="center">The Conflict Dynamic Model</td></tr>
<tr><td colspan="2" align="center">Precipitating Event/Hot Buttons</td></tr>
<tr><td colspan="2" align="center">Initiate Conflict</td></tr>
<tr><td>Constructive Responses
Active
Perspective Taking (PT)
Creating Solutions (CS)
Expressing Emotions (EE)
Reaching Out (RE)</td><td>Destructive Responses
Active
Winning at all Costs (WI)
Displaying Anger (DA)
Demeaning Others (DO)
Retaliating (RE)</td></tr>
<tr><td>Passive
Reflective Thinking (RT)
Delay Responding (DL)
Adapting (AD)</td><td>Passive
Avoiding (AV)
Yielding (YL)
Hiding Emotions (HE)
Self-Criticizing (SC)</td></tr>
<tr><td>Task-Focused Conflict
Focus on task and problem-solving
Positive affect
Tension decreases
Group functioning improves
Conflict De-Escalates</td><td>Person-Focused Conflict
Focus on personalities
Negative affect
Tension increases
Group functioning derailed
Conflict Escalates</td></tr>
</table>

Figure 1. Capobianco et al., 2008b, p. 5.

Another aspect to conflict is its development into either cognitive or emotional conflict. Cognitive conflict focuses on ideas. This conflict is not bad, and as such, may result in instances of productivity or group creativity. Cognitive conflict is often the best type of conflict to engage in because the source of the conflict is the issues, not individual personalities (Capobianco et al., 2008a, p. 3). By contrast, emotional conflict focuses less on the issues and more on personalities, which creates negative emotions for all parties involved. Unlike cognitive conflict, emotional conflict leads to low group functioning, along with the potential to spiral out of control. Emotional conflict is the worst possible conflict that may occur (Capobianco et al., 2008a, p. 3).

The CDP-I instrument categorizes conflict responses based on whether the conflicts themselves are constructive or destructive, the subsequent responses are active or passive, and whether the conflict will develop into an emotional or cognitive scenario. As a result, the emotional responses are divided into four categories: active-constructive, passive-constructive, active-destructive, and passive-destructive (Capobianco et al., 2008a, p. 3).

Active-Constructive Conflict. Active constructive responses, as aforementioned, involve overt actions that individuals take in response to conflict. These behaviors may result in the conflict developing into a constructive conflict, as opposed to an emotional one (Capobianco et al., 2008a, p. 4). Four active-constructive responses are measured (p. 4). The first response is perspective taking. This response involves placing oneself in the position of the other party and understanding their point of views. The second response is known as creating solutions. Here, the individual responds to conflict through brainstorming ideas with the other parties and trying to come up with meaningful ways to solve the problems associated with the conflict. The third response, expressing emotions, involves discussing honest feelings with the other party. Finally, the fourth active-constructive response is reaching out, in which one party makes the first move towards resolving the conflict.

Passive-Constructive Responses. Passive-constructive responses involve conflicting parties responding to a conflict in less active ways. Some ways may include making decisions to refrain from acting, which may provide some eventual benefit to the conflict (Capobianco et al., 2008a, p. 4). As with active-constructive responses, passive-constructive responses have the potential of resulting in a constructive conflict (p. 4). Three passive-constructive responses are reflective thinking, delaying responding, and adapting (p. 4). First, reflective thinking involves responding to conflict by analyzing the conflict, thinking about the advantages and disadvantages, and deciding on the best response to the conflict. Second, conflicting parties may choose to delay responding, which means letting things settle down, waiting, or taking a time out. This is especially helpful when emotions are at a high level. Finally, parties may practice adapting, which is to stay flexible and making the best of a situation.

Active-Destructive Responses. Active-destructive responses are those in which individuals take active roles in a conflict that may result in negative responses, leading to destructive consequences (Capobianco et al., 2008a, p. 5). These negative responses may turn the conflict towards the path of an emotional conflict (p. 5). That means the conflict will focus less of the issues and more on the personalities of the individuals. There are four active-destructive responses, which are winning at all costs, displaying anger, demeaning others, and retaliating (Capobianco et al., 2008a, p. 5). First, winning at all costs means that that individual will argue his/her position intensely, trying to win at all costs. Second, individuals may respond by displaying anger, which includes raising one's voice and using harsh language. Third, an individual may respond to conflict by demeaning others. This response involves being sarcastic towards the other party, laughter, or ridicule. Finally, a person may retaliate by seeking revenge or blocking the other person.

Passive-Destructive Responses. Passive-destructive responses are a less active approach to conflict by not responding in a certain way. The lack of response may lead to a conflict not being handled in a satisfactory manner (Capobianco et al., 2008a, p. 5). Four passive-destructive responses are avoiding, yielding, hiding emotions, and self-criticizing (p. 5). First, avoiding involves individuals acting distant to each other or ignoring each other. Second, individuals may yield, which means that they surrender to the other party in order to avoid more conflict. Third, individuals may hide emotions, even though they are troubled by the conflict. Finally, individuals may self-criticize, which means that they replay the incident over and over, sometimes faulting themselves for the conflict.

Hot Button Responses. Besides the aforementioned four categories, the CDP-I instrument also measures hot buttons, which are emotions that tend to elicit extreme responses such as irritation (Capobianco et al., 2008a, p. 6). The instrument measures how irritated people get when exposed to people who exhibit these behaviors. Capobianco, Davis, and Kraus (2008a) identified nine hot button behaviors.

The first hot button deals with people who display unreliability. These individuals tend to miss deadlines and generally cannot be relied upon to do anything. The second hot button behavior deals with people who display overly-analytical behavior. These individuals tend to focus a great deal on minor issues. The third category of people is those who act unappreciatively. These people do not credit or give praise to others. The fourth behavior is exhibited by people who act aloof. Aloof people tend to be very hard to approach. These individuals also tend to isolate themselves from other people. Fifth, people who micro-manage are those who check up on the progress of others constantly.

Sixth, people who act self-centered are those who believe that they are right all of the time. Seventh, people displaying abrasive behavior are described as those who are abrasive or arrogant. Eighth, people who act untrustworthy tend to exploit the work of others or claim credit for something that they did not do. Finally, people displaying hostility are those who exhibit anger or lose tempers (Capobianco et al., 2008a, p. 6).

Hot button behaviors have the potential to escalate a conflict into a destructive one, which may lead to an emotional conflict. Measuring these emotions is based on the idea that when people learn from upsetting situations, they are more likely to avoid becoming involved in further conflicts (Capobianco et al., 2008a, p. 6).

Reliability of the CDP. The reliability of the CDP is based on both internal and test-retest reliability. The internal reliability coefficients (alpha coefficients) were measured from 9,318 respondents and their raters (Capobianco et al., 2008b, p. 18). The ratings involved behaviors from all 15 conflict responses across the four domains: active-constructive, passive-constructive, active-destructive, and passive-destructive. Internal reliability was also calculated for the hot button responses. According to Capobianco et al. (2008b), the internal reliability was acceptable. Alpha coefficients exceeded .70% of the time, while alpha coefficients exceeding .80 occurred over 50% of the time (Capobianco et al., 2008b, p. 18). As with conflict responses, the hot button responses were acceptable, with alpha coefficients above .70 (Capobianco et al., 2008b, p. 19).

When retesting the 15 conflict responses, the CDP was given to 83 undergraduate college students at two times, which ranged in interval from 77 to 91 days. According to the research, there was positive correlation between the results from the first and second days of testing (Capobianco et al., 2008b, p. 19). In other words, people tend to display certain responses to conflict over several weeks. The lowest associations were for active-destructive, in which the associations indicate that these behaviors occurred at a low frequency. This low frequency may be because active-destructive behaviors are less stable over time and are most likely influenced by provocation from other parties (p. 19).

Validity of the CDP. In terms of validity, the CDP has been analyzed for its relationship to two measures of social desirability, which are part of the Balanced Inventory of Desirable Responding (BIDR). One scale, self-Deception, determines the inflated viewpoints of people's rationality and judgment. The other scale, Impression Management, measures the concern for how one person makes an impression on other people (Capobianco et al., 2008b, p. 20). The differences in correlations between the CDP and the BIDR scales were .20, which indicated a significant difference. However, the differences were small. In other words, the CDP did not have serious issues in terms of social desirability. The scores of the CDP were also more associated with the Self-Deception scale of the BIDR (Capobianco et al., 2008b, p. 21).

When the validity was evaluated in terms of correlation across domains, the active-constructive and passive-constructive responses were more positively associated than the responses in the active-destructive and passive-destructive domains. In fact, some of the associations between active-destructive and passive-destructive responses were near zero (Capobianco et al., 2008b, p. 23).

Another way of measuring the validity of the CDP is comparing respondents who rated themselves versus ratings that were made by their bosses, peers, and direct reports. Again, over 9000 respondents were rated on the fifteen response behaviors (Capobianco et al., 2008b, p. 23). According to the results, each correlation was positive and statistically significant. The ratings were the same across rater categories and behavioral response categories. The only pattern that was different was active-destructive behavior. That behavior was stronger than the other behavioral domains (Capobianco et al., 2008b, p. 24).

The CDP-I was chosen by the author for several reasons. First, the CDP can measure a person's behavior by describing how that person feels before, during, and after a conflict. Also, the CDP allows an assessment of how the individual, as well as bosses and peers, feel before, during, and after a conflict (Capobianco et al., 2008b, p. 7). Furthermore, the CDP gives a complete conflict profile of an individual by offering feedback five aspects. First, the CDP focuses on behaviors that may provoke a reactive behavior, or hot buttons. Second, the CDP examines how the individual typically responds to conflict. Third, the CDP looks at how other people view that individual as he/she responds to conflict. Fourth, the CDP examines the Dynamic Conflict Sequence, which is defined as how individuals respond before, during and after conflict. Fifth, the CDP measures which conflict responses can harm a person's position in the organization, which is called Organizational Perspective on Conflict (Capobianco et al., 2008b, p. 7). The researcher was impressed with the thoroughness of the CDP, and thus selected the instrument. Also, the CDP was the culmination of two years of revision and testing. The first version was written in the spring of 1998 and was revised two more times, until a final version (the present CDP) was accepted (Capobianco et al., 2008b, pp. 9, 13).

The researcher found that the CDP has several applications. According the Capobianco, Davis, and Kraus (2008a), the CDP can be used for conflict resolution (resolving specific conflict issues), leadership development (handling conflict effectively), career development/individual coaching (helping to move into demanding career roles), or team building (conducting team intervention to build cohesiveness) (Capobianco et al., 2008a, pp. 10-11).

Data Collection and Methods

Unit of Analysis. The unit of analysis is the individual. The idea is that all students within a community college count. By examining the individual, the researcher studied the students' response to situations of conflict.

The Sample Size. The sample size was limited to 150 community college students throughout the United States of America. Also, sampling was accomplished using simple random sampling, which is the most basic form of probability sampling. Probability sampling allows researchers to "specify for each case in the population the probability of its inclusion in the sample" (Frankfort-Nachmias & Leon-Guerrero, 2006, p. 348). As such, simple random sampling is defined as "a sample design chosen in such a way as to ensure that 1) every member of the population has an equal chance of being chosen and 2) every combination of N members has an equal chance of being chosen" (Frankfort-Nachmias & Leon-Guerrero, 2006, pp. 348-349).

The research involved inferential statistics, which concerns itself with making predictions about populations from observations and analysis of a sample (Frankfort-Nachmias & Leon-Guerrero, 2006, p. 17). In other words, the research will be quantitative. The author distributed needs assessments, which, according to Beebe (2004) as a means of "finding out what learners don't know or can't do what they should know or do in order to perform their job" (p. 51). The type of needs assessment that was conducted consisted of a questionnaire, which is a series of questions that seeks responses to learn about knowledge, attitude, or behavior (Beebe, 2004, p. 51). The type of questionnaire that the researcher utilized was the CDP, more specifically, the CDP-Individual (CDP-I).

Capobianco et al. (2008a) distinguished between two types of CDP questionnaires, CDP-I and CDP-360. The CDP-I, or CDP-Individual, is used to measure conflict responses at an individual. It is, according to Capobianco, Davis, and Kraus, a "self-report" (2008a, p. 13). On the other hand, the CDP-360 is much more extensive. The researcher decided to use the CDP-I due to the fact that it focuses on the individual and that it is far less expensive choice than the CDP-360.

The CDP-I questionnaire was written in a combination of Likert-scale, which measures degree of agreement, and multiple-choice, which involves asking a question and offering limited choices (Beebe, 2004, p. 52, 55).

The questions themselves were derived from the CDP-I individual test, which was devised by the Center for Conflict Dynamics at Eckerd College (St. Petersburg, Florida). The first set of questions that the respondents answered consisted of four demographic questions: age, ethnicity, gender, and social background. The CDP-I questionnaire itself consisted of 99 questions describing ways in which an individual may act during conflicts (Eckerd College CDP Questionnaire, 2009, p. 1). Responses to these questions were used to measure the dependent variable, which consisted of individual responses to conflict. The respondents rated the frequency of responses by using a five-point scale (1=Never, 2=Rarely, 3=Sometimes, 4=Often, 5=Almost Always). As for hot button responses, the respondents used a five-point scale. This time, the degree to which the individual is upset is ranked as (1=Not At All, 2=A Little, 3=Moderately, 4=Considerably, 5=Extremely) (Capobianco et al., 2008b).

The researcher took a short course from Eckerd College in July 2011 from Craig Runde, the Director of the Conflict Dynamics Profile. The researcher was certified to administer the CDP-I on July 28, 2011. After certification, the researcher wrote the proposal on the dissertation research and presented it in November 2011. After passing the proposal defense, the researcher submitted an Institutional Review (IRB) Protocol Form to the IRB representative in the Graduate School of Social Sciences (SHSS) at Nova Southeastern University. In addition to the IRB protocol, the researcher submitted a sample of the questionnaire, a sample of the consent letter (see Appendix B), and a demographic survey meant to collect the independent variables (see Appendix C). Since the researcher was conducting an online survey, the researcher was required to submit an IRB form. The researcher was approved for the study on April 18, 2012 by Dr. Pat Cole.

After approval of the IRB forms, the researcher contacted a survey website of a survey service called Zoomerang (zoomerang.com). Zoomerang contains information on community college students previously sampled from other surveys. Before administering the survey to the 150 community college students, a pilot study consisting of the CDP-I survey was administered to 25 respondents. The purpose if the pilot study was to determine if students are able to successfully complete the questionnaires. The researcher sent an introductory email, reminding the participants that the survey was a pilot study and for the purposes of that study. Through this process, the researcher was able to uncover any mistakes in the process of administering the study.

Of the 25 respondents who were sent the study via email, 11 respondents completed the study. When determining issues with the survey, some respondents emailed the researcher and stated that they could not type their responses to the survey. Also, some people did not receive their surveys via email when it was deployed. The researcher found that certain browsers, such as Google Chrome or Mozilla Firefox, work best with the survey. In terms of analysis, the low number of responses was not enough for a representative sample. Thus, the results were not analyzed using inferential statistics. However, the Zoomerang service was able to analyze the results and to compile the results into Microsoft Excel worksheets.

Once the Zoomerang account was created, the researcher utilized the service to randomly select 150 community college students from throughout the United States. The students selected through Zoomerang were granted access to the CDP-I questionnaire site by the researcher. The researcher administered the online test from Zoomerang.com. Since the survey is anonymous, participants were not required to provide their names to the researcher.

The first page of the survey that the students received was the participation letter, which invited community college students to take the Conflict-Dynamic Profile-Individual survey. The letter explained the purpose of the study, the demographic range of the potential participants, the type of survey instrument used, possibility of the study being recorded, any risks or benefits, possible use of academic data, the right to refuse participation, and electronic verification. Since the survey is online, the participants gave their consent by clicking on AGREE or DISAGREE if they refuse to participate. The next page was a screening page (see Appendix D), which asked if the respondents were community college students. Respondents who answered YES proceeded to the next page, which contained a demographic survey. The demographic survey asked for the participant's age, ethnicity, gender, and socioeconomic background. After finishing the demographic questions page, the students clicked NEXT to proceed to the CDP-I instrument.

The data from the CDP-I questionnaires were compiled into frequency tables using frequency distribution, which Frankfort-Nachmias and Leon-Guerrero defined as "a table reporting the number of observations falling into each category of the variable" (2006, p. 28). Frequency tables were constructed using SPSS version 15 for Windows. The data sets to be utilized were the result of the data collected from all responses from Zoomerang.

To ensure that coding the results will be fairly simple, the author compiled the number of answers for every question. Coding was necessary because every response affects the outcome of the study. Because the screening page was placed on the first page of the CDP-I on Zoomerang, the author needed to code all the responses in order to alleviate confusion and to ensure that the correct responses were placed in the proper table. In addition, abbreviations of demographic questions and conflict response behaviors were necessary to reduce space in the Excel Worksheet. The abbreviations were simple and corresponded to each category.

For example, the demographic questions consisted of age, ethnicity, gender, and socioeconomic background. In the case of age, the code AGE was used to represent the independent variable of age, while the code ETHNICITY was used to represent the independent variable of ethnicity. Also, the code GENDER was used to represent the independent variable of gender, while the code INCOME was used to represent the independent variable of socioeconomic background (annual family income).

As for the dependent variable of responses to conflict, the responses were coded by response type, response, and question number on the CDP-I. For instance, the active-constructive response of perspective taking for question 10 of the CDP-I was coded as A-C-PERSPTAKIN-10.

To protect the confidentiality of the respondents, the researcher stored the pin numbers and survey results on a password-protected computer. Thirty-six months after the conclusion of the study, all data associated with the research will be destroyed.

Data Analysis

To analyze the difference between two groups' responses to the behavioral CDP questions the researcher used t-test for independent samples. Assumptions for this type of test include:

- each group is considered to be a sample from a distinct population

- the responses in each group are independent of those in the other group

- the distributions of the variable of interest are normal

$$t = \frac{\bar{x}_1 - \bar{x}_2}{\sqrt{(s_1^2 / n_1 + s_2^2 / n_2)}}$$

Where:

$$\bar{x} = 1/n\ (x_1 + x_2 + x_3 \dots\dots + x_n) = (1/n)\ \Sigma x_i$$

$n = $ **sample size**

$s^2 = 1/(n-1)\ [(x_1 - \bar{x})^2 + (x_2 - \bar{x})^2 + \dots\dots + (x_n - \bar{x})^2]$ **(long formula)**

$s^2 = 1/(n-1)\ [\Sigma x_i^2 - (1/n)(\Sigma x_i)^2]$ **(hand calculation formula)**

$k = n_1 - 1$ **or** $n_2 - 1$**, whichever is less (if** $n_1 \neq n_2$**)**

$k = n_1 + n_2 - 2$ **(if** $n_1 = n_2$**)**

To test if more than 2 population means are equal, the researcher will use One –Way ANOVA. The logic used in ANOVA to compare means of multiple groups is similar to that used with the t-test to compare means of two independent groups. The assumptions needed for the t-test are also needed for ANOVA. We need to assume:

- random, independent sampling from the k populations;

- normal population distributions;

- equal variances within the k populations

The logic of this approach extends directly to one-way analysis of variance with *k* groups. First, the estimates of the population variance are calculated: one is the pooled variance of scores within groups, and the other is based on the observed variance between group means. These two estimates are expected to be equal if the population means are equal for all k groups, but the estimates are expected to differ if the population means are not all the same. The test statistic is the **F-test**

$$F(df_{BG}, df_{WG}) = \frac{Between\ Groups\ estimate\ of\ \sigma_y^2}{Within\ Groups\ estimate\ of\ \sigma_y^2} = \frac{MS_{WG}}{MS_{BG}}$$

For purposes of the quantitative analysis, a critical factor of the CDP scoring system is that it has been mathematically standardized to yield interval-ratio data that could be readily tested using conventional statistical methods (Capobianco et al., 2008b). All fifteen behavioral parameters shown and Hot Button scores are standardized to "define an average score as 50 with a standard deviation of 10 points" (Capobianco et al., 2008b). Therefore, all responses of participants were standardized. Analysis of all the data was conducted using Microsoft Excel 7 and using SPSS vs. 19.

Chapter 4: Data Analysis and Presentation

Introduction

This chapter presents the data analyses starting with the contributions of the pilot study. Then data analysis focuses on the results for the 150 participant survey conducted via Zoomerang to test the study hypotheses. Descriptive and inferential statistics are presented. The T-test is used to test the difference between two groups. Analysis of Variance is used to test the difference when there are more than two groups.

Pilot Study Demographic Analysis

In the pilot study, participants were invited to complete the CDP-I survey instrument and to offer feedback so that the researcher could make improvements to the research design. The researcher emailed the survey to 25 volunteer students. Out of the 25 respondents, 11 completed the survey. Some respondents indicated that they could not complete the survey because the survey was unresponsive. The researcher found that the browser used by some respondents may have been out of date. As a result, the researcher added a disclaimer page explaining that the respondents' computer should include recent versions of Internet Explorer, Mozilla Firefox, or Chrome. That page was placed before the beginning of the survey.

Another respondent mentioned a spelling error on one of the survey questions, which was corrected by the researcher. Finally, another respondent suggested that the researcher increase the choices under the ethnicity category. The previous choices included African-American, Caucasian, Asian-American, Latino, and Other. The respondent changed the categories to African-American, European-American (Non-Hispanic), Hispanic, Asian/Pacific Islander, and Other ethnicity.

Demographic Variables Descriptive Analysis

In the national community college study, 150 respondents completed the CDP-I survey instrument. The researcher made another change to the ethnicity question and added more categories in order for the survey to become more inclusive. Thus, the ethnic categories included African-American, European-American (Non-Hispanic), Hispanic, Asian/Pacific Islander, Alaskan Native/Native American, Two or More Ethnicities, and Other Ethnicity.

Age. The demographic data of the national community college study yielded the following results. In terms of age, of the 150 respondents who participated in the pilot study, 131 of the respondents (87%) were between the ages of 18-24. This age group represented the highest percentage of respondents. Next, 9 respondents (6%) were in the 25-34 age group. In addition, 4 respondents from the 35-44 age group (3%), 4 respondents from the 45-54 age group (3%), and 2 respondents from the 55-65 age group (1%) answered the survey (Zoomerang.com, 2012b).

Previous research into age indicated that the average age of community college students is 28 (American Association of Community Colleges, 2011). Maxwell et al. (2003, p. 25) and Palazesi and Bower (2006, p. 45) indicated that 16% of community college students are older than 40 years old. Also, Calgagno et al. (2007) found that 35% of full-time community college students who enrolled in the Fall of 2002 were between 25-65 years old (p. 218). The national study yielded significantly different results, with 87% of the respondents belonging to the 18-24 age group. This is much lower than the average age of community college students, which was 28 (Zoomerang.com, 2012b).

Thus, the study indicated that a greater number of younger students are enrolling in community colleges.

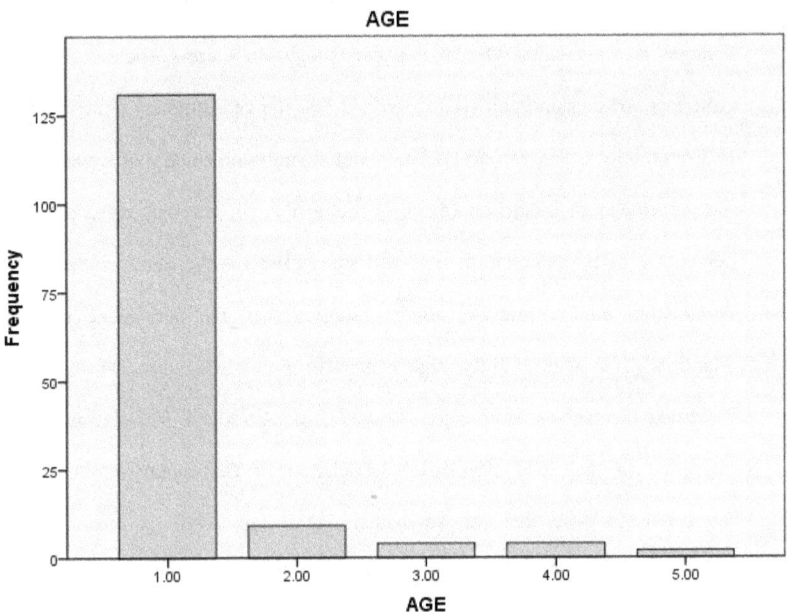

Figure 2. Age distribution.

Ethnicity. In terms of ethnicity, the highest number of respondents, 67 (45%), identified themselves as European-American (Non-Hispanic). Also, 26 (17%) were Other Ethnicity, while 24 (16%) of respondents identified themselves as Hispanic. In addition, 18 respondents (12%) identified themselves as African-American, and 11 respondents (7%) were Asian/Pacific Islander. Furthermore, 4 respondents (3%) identified themselves as Two or More Ethnicities. Finally, No one identified as Alaskan Native/Native American (Zoomerang.com, 2012b).

As for ethnicity, previous research indicated that 45% of students in community colleges are minorities. Out of that percentage, 16% are Hispanic, 13% are African-American, 6% Asian/Pacific Islander, and 1% Native American (American Association of Community Colleges, 2011). The national study indicated that when added together, the percentage of minorities (52%) is higher than in previous research. However, the percentage of Hispanics in the national study (16%) is the same as the 2011 American Association of Community Colleges study. Also, the percentage of Asian/Pacific Islanders (7%) was slightly higher than in previous studies. Furthermore, no one identified themselves as Alaskan Native/Native American. This is lower than the 1% identified in the 2011 American Association of Community College Study. It is interesting to note that the researcher found that 17% of respondents identified themselves as Other Ethnicity, and that 3% were Two or More Ethnicities (Zoomerang.com, 2012b). Very little research has been conducted on people who identify themselves as other or multiple ethnicities. The results indicated that community college students are becoming increasingly diverse, and that more students are identifying themselves as other ethnicities.

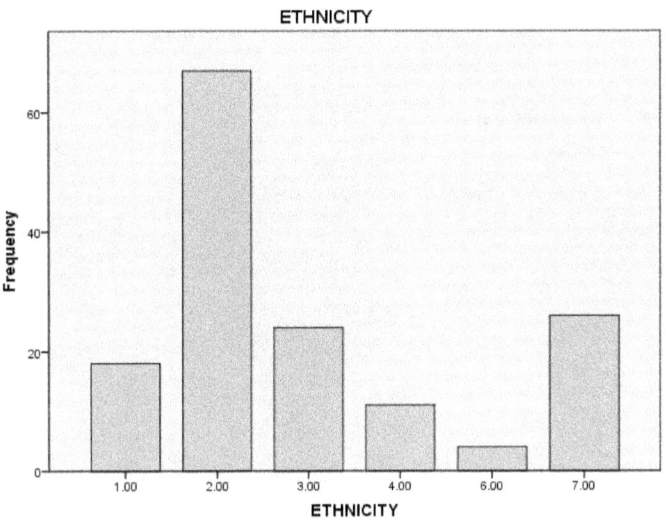

Figure 3. Ethnicity distribution.

Gender. As far as gender was concerned, 78 (52%) of the respondents were men, while 70 respondents (47%) of the respondents were women. Only 2 respondents (1%) identified themselves as Other Gender (Zoomerang.com, 2012b). In terms of gender, previous research from the American Association of Community Colleges indicated that 58% of community college students are female and 42% are male (2011). The percentage of women in the study is significantly lower than in previous studies. Thus, the research indicated that more men than women are in community colleges today.

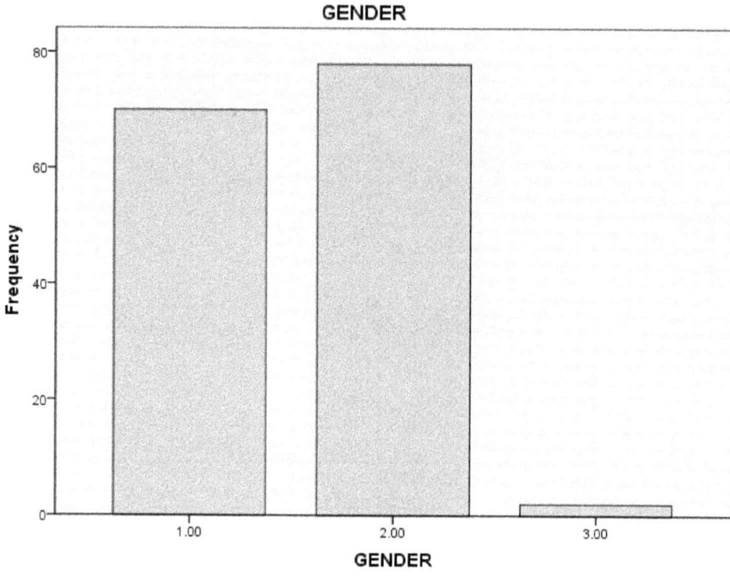

Figure 4. Gender distribution.

Socioeconomic Background. In terms of socioeconomic background (Annual Family Income), the highest number of respondents, 65 (43%), came from families with an annual income of $20,001-$59,999. The next highest number of respondents, 44 (29%), came from families with an annual income of $1-$20,000. Also, 23 respondents (15%) came from a family earning an annual income of $60,000-$99,000. Finally, 18 respondents (12%) came from a family earning an annual income of $100,000 or above (Zoomerang.com, 2012b).

Previous research concerning socioeconomic background indicated that 59% of community college students are part-time employees and that 42% of them are on financial aid (American Association of Community Colleges, 2011). According to the results from the national study, a greater percentage of the respondents (45%) came from relatively higher-income families than from lower-income families (29%) (Zoomerang.com, 2012b). Thus, the study indicated that more community college students are coming from families earning higher incomes than previously recorded.

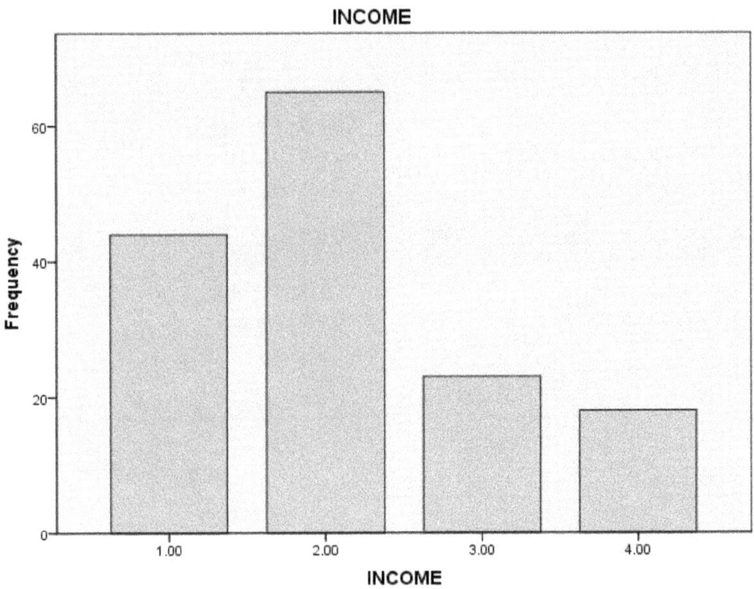

Figure 5. Income distribution.

The demographic data results from the national study were placed into frequency tables. The raw numbers of respondents were converted to percentages. Both numbers were placed into the frequency tables.

Dependent Variables

Database from the Zoomerang engine was converted to an Excel Spreadsheet to start the data analysis for the CDP scale scores. Results from each question were arranged according to the CDP constructive conflict, destructive conflict, and hot button profiles (Capobianco et al., 2008c).

CONSTRUCTIVE BEHAVIORS		DESTRUCTIVE BEHAVIORS
1. Perspective Taking (PT) 2. Creating Solutions (CS) 3. Expressing Emotions (EE) 4. Reaching Out (RO)	A C T I V E	1. Winning at All Costs (WI) 2. Displaying Anger (DA) 3. Demeaning Others (DO) 4. Retaliating (RE)
5. Reflective Thinking (RT) 6. Delay Responding (DR) 7. Adapting (AD)	P A S S I V E	5. Avoiding (AV) 6. Yielding (YL) 7. Hiding Emotions (HE) 8. Self Criticizing (SC)
HOT BUTTONS		
Unreliable 2. Over-Analytical 3. Unappreciative 4. Aloof		5. 5 Micro-Managing 6. Self-Centered 7. Abrasive 8. Untrustworthy 9. Hostile

Figure 6. Behaviors and hot buttons assessed by the Conflict Dynamics Profile.

The responses were added for each behavior and then standardized so they could be compared among the different groups. The standardized scores allow a comparison between a participant's behavior versus that of his or her peers (Capobianco et al., 2008,

p. 5). According to the authors, average T scores tended to be 50. One-half of people scored below 50, while the other half of people scored above 50 (p. 5). The T scores range from 0 to 100, with 68% of scores falling between 40 and 60. The T scores can be ranked as very low, low, average, high, or very high (p. 5). The CDP chart lists the T score ranges for responses to conflict according to the following: Very low T scores are below 40, low T scores range from 40-45, average T scores range from 45-55, high T scores range from 55 to 60, and very high T scores range from 60 to 70.

These scales are used to measure both active and passive constructive responses, active and passive destructive responses, and hot-button responses. However, the scales for response categories are interpreted differently. For example, higher ratings of constructive responses are more desirable than lower scores (Capobianco et al., 2008d, p. 7). In contrast, lower ratings of destructive responses are more desirable (Capobianco et al., 2008d, p. 10). Likewise, lower ratings among hot button responses mean that respondents do not possess negative emotions that can increase conflicts (Capobianco et al. 2008a, p. 6; Capobianco et al., 2008d, p. 19). Tables detailing sample scores of active-constructive, passive-destructive, active-destructive, passive-destructive, and hot button responses are found in Appendix A.

Table *1*

Descriptive Statistics for CDP Scale Scores

Descriptive Statistics

	N	Minimum	Maximum	Mean	Std. Deviation
PT	150	17.60	70.93	48.7560	7.84807
CS	150	4.07	71.86	41.5543	10.41059
EE	150	18.84	62.32	36.1838	9.08723
RO	150	-1.18	77.25	41.1115	15.19170
RT	150	1.69	69.49	33.9830	11.19147
DR	150	7.14	88.78	50.7492	12.97211
AD	150	-1.92	75.00	38.1540	14.29600
WI	150	23.83	90.50	51.7778	12.57507
DA	150	33.93	99.51	68.4148	9.99649
DO	150	38.04	109.46	73.2145	11.51769
RE	150	40.38	115.85	78.1447	11.85382
AV	150	31.52	92.12	60.6314	9.73610
YL	150	29.08	90.62	57.0780	12.28515
HE	150	22.19	84.69	59.0895	10.12507
SC	150	19.35	71.30	44.8035	8.00646
HBUNR	150	9.86	64.66	38.6749	11.01794
HBOA	150	30.15	90.76	64.5951	12.47005
HBUNA	150	23.63	73.63	52.5659	11.88397
HBAL	150	22.12	82.73	54.5703	10.75385
HBMI	150	27.83	76.02	51.6867	10.05665
HBSE	150	21.84	74.47	51.0547	10.16226
HBAB	150	19.05	73.11	45.7652	10.53437
HBUNT	150	4.85	63.68	36.0042	13.37993
HBHO	150	15.19	67.14	40.3473	9.47281
Valid N (listwise)	150				

Hypotheses Testing

Inferential statistics were used to examine the hypotheses of the study. To analyze the difference between the two groups' responses to the behavioral CDP questions the researcher used the t-test for independent samples. One-way analysis of variance (ANOVA) was used to test the difference among variable categories and conflict dynamic profile scale scores. For the purposes of the research, the alpha level, or the level of probability at which the null hypothesis can be rejected, was set at .05. If the probability for each response is below .05, then the response would be considered significant, and the null hypothesis could be rejected. However, if the probability for each response was above .05, then the null hypothesis cannot be rejected.

Age

H1:   Students of different ages will have different responses to CDP scale scores.

The ANOVA analysis was performed for age, for each of the CDP scale scores. According to Table 2, there is no significant difference in age when it came to responses to conflict. For example, the response for creating solutions, CS, was .834, far higher than the set level of significance of .05. As a result, responding by creating solutions is not a significant factor by age group. Thus, the null hypothesis for age cannot be rejected.

Table *2*

ANOVA for AGE Constructive and Destructive Responses to Conflict

ANOVA

DV		Sum of Squares	df	Mean Square	F	Sig.
PT	Between Groups	219.68	4.00	54.92	0.89	0.47
	Within Groups	8957.56	145.00	61.78		
	Total	9177.24	149.00			
CS	Between Groups	160.74	4.00	40.19	0.36	0.83
	Within Groups	15987.94	145.00	110.26		
	Total	16148.68	149.00			
EE	Between Groups	150.80	4.00	37.70	0.45	0.77
	Within Groups	12153.29	145.00	83.82		
	Total	12304.09	149.00			
RO	Between Groups	205.62	4.00	51.40	0.22	0.93
	Within Groups	34181.74	145.00	235.74		
	Total	34387.36	149.00			
RT	Between Groups	448.73	4.00	112.18	0.89	0.47
	Within Groups	18213.39	145.00	125.61		
	Total	18662.12	149.00			
DR	Between Groups	356.25	4.00	89.06	0.52	0.72
	Within Groups	24716.82	145.00	170.46		
	Total	25073.07	149.00			
AD	Between Groups	1004.63	4.00	251.16	1.24	0.30
	Within Groups	29447.35	145.00	203.09		
	Total	30451.98	149.00			
WI	Between Groups	611.12	4.00	152.78	0.97	0.43
	Within Groups	22950.60	145.00	158.28		
	Total	23561.71	149.00			
DA	Between Groups	427.66	4.00	106.91	1.07	0.37
	Within Groups	14461.88	145.00	99.74		
	Total	14889.54	149.00			
DO	Between Groups	270.61	4.00	67.65	0.50	0.73
	Within Groups	19495.31	145.00	134.45		
	Total	19765.91	149.00			
RE	Between Groups	527.11	4.00	131.78	0.94	0.45
	Within Groups	20409.32	145.00	140.75		
	Total	20936.43	149.00			

AV	Between Groups	198.09	4.00	49.52	0.52	0.72
	Within Groups	13925.87	145.00	96.04		
	Total	14123.95	149.00			
YL	Between Groups	535.27	4.00	133.82	0.88	0.48
	Within Groups	21952.54	145.00	151.40		
	Total	22487.81	149.00			
HE	Between Groups	31.80	4.00	7.95	0.08	0.99
	Within Groups	15243.24	145.00	105.13		
	Total	15275.04	149.00			
SC	Between Groups	153.77	4.00	38.44	0.59	0.67
	Within Groups	9397.64	145.00	64.81		
	Total	9551.40	149.00			

A one-way ANOVA was performed for age and Hot Button responses. Table 3 shows no significant differences among age groups for hot button responses. For example, the response for unreliability, HBUNR, was .530, far higher than the set level of significance of .05. As a result, the response to people displaying unreliable behaviors is not a significant factor by age group. Thus, the null hypothesis for age cannot be rejected.

Table *3*

One-way ANOVA for AGE and Hot Button Responses

ANOVA

		Sum of Squares	Df	Mean Square	F	Sig.
HBUNR	Between Groups	388.45	4.00	97.11	0.80	0.53
	Within Groups	17699.41	145.00	122.07		
	Total	18087.87	149.00			
HBOA	Between Groups	758.99	4.00	189.75	1.23	0.30
	Within Groups	22410.84	145.00	154.56		
	Total	23169.83	149.00			
HBUNA	Between Groups	536.33	4.00	134.08	0.95	0.44

	Within Groups	20506.75	145.00	141.43		
	Total	21043.08	149.00			
HBAL	Between Groups	504.50	4.00	126.13	1.09	0.36
	Within Groups	16726.65	145.00	115.36		
	Total	17231.15	149.00			
HBMI	Between Groups	289.47	4.00	72.37	0.71	0.59
	Within Groups	14779.84	145.00	101.93		
	Total	15069.31	149.00			
HBSE	Between Groups	177.15	4.00	44.29	0.42	0.79
	Within Groups	15210.30	145.00	104.90		
	Total	15387.45	149.00			
HBAB	Between Groups	773.64	4.00	193.41	1.78	0.14
	Within Groups	15761.34	145.00	108.70		
	Total	16534.97	149.00			
HBUNT	Between Groups	339.86	4.00	84.97	0.47	0.76
	Within Groups	26334.48	145.00	181.62		
	Total	26674.34	149.00			
HBHO	Between Groups	276.42	4.00	69.11	0.77	0.55
	Within Groups	13093.97	145.00	90.30		
	Total	13370.40	149.00			

Ethnicity

H2:   Students of different ethnicities will have different responses to CDP scale scores.

A one-way ANOVA was performed for ethnicity. There were no significant differences between ethnicities when it comes to responses to conflict. Therefore, ethnicity is not a factor in response to conflict, and, thus, the null hypothesis for ethnicity cannot be rejected.

Table *4*

One-way ANOVA for Ethnicity and Constructive and Destructive Responses to Conflict

ANOVA

		Sum of Squares	df	Mean Square	F	Sig.
PT	Between Groups	532.78	5.00	106.56	1.78	0.12
	Within Groups	8644.46	144.00	60.03		
	Total	9177.24	149.00			
CS	Between Groups	733.44	5.00	146.69	1.37	0.24
	Within Groups	15415.24	144.00	107.05		
	Total	16148.68	149.00			
EE	Between Groups	520.37	5.00	104.08	1.27	0.28
	Within Groups	11783.71	144.00	81.83		
	Total	12304.09	149.00			
RO	Between Groups	638.11	5.00	127.62	0.55	0.74
	Within Groups	33749.25	144.00	234.37		
	Total	34387.36	149.00			
RT	Between Groups	1040.64	5.00	208.13	1.70	0.14
	Within Groups	17621.47	144.00	122.37		
	Total	18662.12	149.00			
DR	Between Groups	155.33	5.00	31.07	0.18	0.97
	Within Groups	24917.74	144.00	173.04		
	Total	25073.07	149.00			
AD	Between Groups	541.97	5.00	108.39	0.52	0.76
	Within Groups	29910.01	144.00	207.71		

	Total	30451.98	149.00			
WI	Between Groups	841.37	5.00	168.27	1.07	0.38
	Within Groups	22720.34	144.00	157.78		
	Total	23561.71	149.00			
DA	Between Groups	582.09	5.00	116.42	1.17	0.33
	Within Groups	14307.45	144.00	99.36		
	Total	14889.54	149.00			
DO	Between Groups	382.47	5.00	76.49	0.57	0.72
	Within Groups	19383.44	144.00	134.61		
	Total	19765.91	149.00			
RE	Between Groups	1425.26	5.00	285.05	2.10	0.07
	Within Groups	19511.18	144.00	135.49		
	Total	20936.43	149.00			
AV	Between Groups	340.93	5.00	68.19	0.71	0.62
	Within Groups	13783.02	144.00	95.72		
	Total	14123.95	149.00			
YL	Between Groups	279.80	5.00	55.96	0.36	0.87
	Within Groups	22208.01	144.00	154.22		
	Total	22487.81	149.00			
HE	Between Groups	444.59	5.00	88.92	0.86	0.51
	Within Groups	14830.45	144.00	102.99		
	Total	15275.04	149.00			
SC	Between Groups	326.68	5.00	65.34	1.02	0.41
	Within Groups	9224.72	144.00	64.06		
	Total	9551.40	149.00			

Table 5 shows the results for ethnicity and hot buttons responses. There was no significant difference in ethnicity when it came to hot button responses. Thus, the null hypothesis for ethnicity cannot be rejected.

Table 5

One-way ANOVA for ETHNICITY for Hot Button Responses

ANOVA

		Sum of Squares	df	Mean Square	F	Sig.
HBUNR	Between Groups	452.54	5.00	90.51	0.74	0.60
	Within Groups	17635.33	144.00	122.47		
	Total	18087.87	149.00			
HBOA	Between Groups	144.18	5.00	28.84	0.18	0.97
	Within Groups	23025.65	144.00	159.90		
	Total	23169.83	149.00			
HBUNA	Between Groups	490.50	5.00	98.10	0.69	0.63
	Within Groups	20552.58	144.00	142.73		
	Total	21043.08	149.00			
HBAL	Between Groups	349.87	5.00	69.97	0.60	0.70
	Within Groups	16881.28	144.00	117.23		
	Total	17231.15	149.00			
HBMI	Between Groups	117.00	5.00	23.40	0.23	0.95
	Within Groups	14952.31	144.00	103.84		
	Total	15069.31	149.00			
HBSE	Between Groups	192.35	5.00	38.47	0.37	0.87
	Within Groups	15195.10	144.00	105.52		
	Total	15387.45	149.00			

HBAB	Between Groups	258.92	5.00	51.79	0.46	0.81
	Within Groups	16276.05	144.00	113.03		
	Total	16534.97	149.00			
HBUNT	Between Groups	671.29	5.00	134.26	0.74	0.59
	Within Groups	26003.06	144.00	180.58		
	Total	26674.34	149.00			
HBHO	Between Groups	318.68	5.00	63.74	0.70	0.62
	Within Groups	13051.72	144.00	90.64		
	Total	13370.40	149.00			

Gender

H3: Students of different genders will have different responses to CDP scale scores.

Table *6*

Group Statistic Concerning Gender Differences in Conflict Responses

Group Statistics

	GENDER	N	Mean	Std. Deviation	Std. Error Mean
PT	1	70	49.55	6.63	0.79
	2	78	48.20	8.79	1.00
CS	1	70	40.87	9.48	1.13
	2	78	42.53	11.07	1.25
EE	1	70	32.66	6.90	0.83
	2	78	39.09	9.73	1.10
RO	1	70	44.90	14.49	1.73
	2	78	37.85	15.29	1.73
RT	1	70	31.90	9.65	1.15
	2	78	35.92	12.21	1.38
DR	1	70	51.90	11.13	1.33
	2	78	49.92	14.44	1.63

AD	1	70	38.46	13.04	1.56
	2	78	37.72	15.55	1.76
WI	1	70	48.77	10.98	1.31
	2	78	54.34	13.49	1.53
DA	1	70	69.00	8.36	1.00
	2	78	68.03	11.37	1.29
DO	1	70	71.90	9.75	1.17
	2	78	74.27	12.95	1.47
RE	1	70	78.32	10.70	1.28
	2	78	78.05	13.00	1.47
AV	1	70	59.11	7.88	0.94
	2	78	62.16	11.06	1.25
YL	1	70	55.78	10.66	1.27
	2	78	58.17	13.69	1.55
HE	1	70	61.42	9.03	1.08
	2	78	57.09	10.76	1.22
SC	1	70	44.67	6.83	0.82
	2	78	44.87	9.03	1.02

Table 6 detailed the average behavioral responses to conflict based on gender and response categories. Group 1 represented females, while Group 2 represented males. A third group that was measured, Group 3, represented other genders. Since only 2 of the 150 respondents identified as other genders, the results were insufficient to perform statistical analyses. Thus, only Groups 1 and 2 were analyzed.

As mentioned in the data analysis section in Chapter 3, all fifteen of the behavioral parameters, as well as the hot button behaviors are standardized to "define an average score as 50 with a standard deviation of 10 points" (Capobianco et al., 2008b). According to Capobianco, Davis, & Kraus (2008a), high scores on constructive responses indicated areas of strength and low scores indicate a need for improvement. However, high scores on destructive responses indicated a need for improvement, whereas low scores indicate areas of strength (Capobianco et al., 2008a, p. 16). If one group scores below the lower threshold score of 45 on a constructive behavioral response, for instance, there would be a need for improvement in how one responds to conflict. Conversely, if a group scored above the upper threshold level 55 on a constructive behavioral response, then the group exhibited strengths in responding to conflict situations (Capobianco et al., 2008a, p. 16).

With respect to the active-constructive response of perspective-taking, females exhibited a higher mean score (49.55) than males (48.20). Both responses were slightly lower than the average response score of 50. In the case of taking perspective, both males and females scored above the lower threshold level of 45 and close to the average score of 50, meaning that they exhibited slightly below-average active-constructive responses to conflict. The standard deviations between the genders were less than the average standard deviation of 10 pts. Females had a lower standard deviation (6.63) than males (8.80), indicating that there was slightly less variation in the distribution of responses among the respondents in the female group when it comes to perspective taking. Also, the standard error of the mean was lower among females (.792) than among males (.995), indicating that there was less dispersion in the sampling distribution of the mean for PT responses for females.

In the passive-constructive response of reflective thinking, RT, females were found to display a lower mean response score of 31.90 than men, 35.92. Both conflict responses were below the average score of 50, but below the threshold level of 45. The scores indicated that both gender groups scored below-average when it came to passive-constructive responses to conflict. In terms of standard deviation, there was less variation in the distribution among females (9.65) than among males (12.21). The male group experienced a higher standard deviation from the average of 10, indicating that there was great variation within the group of respondents. Furthermore, there was less standard error of the mean among females (1.15) than among males (1.38).

In the active-destructive category of winning, WI, the mean response score for females was 48.77, which was lower than that of males (54.34). The males exhibited a mean response score that is higher than the average score of 50, and close to the high threshold score of 55, indicating that the male group may need improvement in how they respond to conflict in a destructive manner. The higher standard deviation among males (13.49) indicated more variation in the group than among females, which had a standard deviation of 10.98. Both gender groups experienced higher than average standard deviation. This could mean that there was a wide variation of responses within each group. Also, the males exhibited a higher standard error of the mean (1.53) than females (1.31), indicating greater dispersion in the sampling distribution of the mean.

In the passive-destructive category of avoiding, AV, the mean responses to conflicts among males (62.16) was higher than the mean responses for females (59.11). Both gender groups exhibited higher tendencies to avoid, which was higher than the average score of 50, indicating that both groups may need to improve how they display passive destructive responses. In terms of standard deviations from the mean, the females exhibited lower than average standard deviations, 7.88, than the males, 11.10. The lower standard deviations among the female group could indicate that there were fewer variations in responses. Also, the males exhibited a higher standard error (1.25) than the females (.94). This could mean that there was less dispersion in the sampling distribution of the mean among females than among males.

Table 7

T-test Gender Constructive and Destructive Responses to Conflict

Independent Samples Test

		t-test for Equality of Means				
		t	df	Sig. (2-tailed)	Mean Difference	Std. Error Difference
PT	EV assumed	1.05	146.00	0.30	1.35	1.29
	EV not assumed	1.06	141.92	0.29	1.35	1.27
CS	EV assumed	-0.97	146.00	0.33	-1.66	1.70
	EV not assumed	-0.98	145.69	0.33	-1.66	1.69
EE	EV assumed	-4.59	146.00	0.00	-6.43	1.40
	EV not assumed	-4.67	138.88	0.00	-6.43	1.38
RO	EV assumed	2.87	146.00	0.01	7.05	2.46
	EV not assumed	2.88	145.56	0.01	7.05	2.45
RT	EV assumed	-2.20	146.00	0.03	-4.02	1.82
	EV not assumed	-2.23	143.76	0.03	-4.02	1.80
DR	EV assumed	0.92	146.00	0.36	1.97	2.14
	EV not assumed	0.94	142.85	0.35	1.97	2.11
AD	EV assumed	0.31	146.00	0.76	0.74	2.37
	EV not assumed	0.32	145.36	0.75	0.74	2.35
WI	EV assumed	-2.73	146.00	0.01	-5.56	2.04
	EV not assumed	-2.76	144.67	0.01	-5.56	2.01
DA	EV assumed	0.59	146.00	0.56	0.97	1.66
	EV not assumed	0.59	140.73	0.55	0.97	1.63
DO	EV assumed	-1.24	146.00	0.22	-2.36	1.90
	EV not assumed	-1.26	141.83	0.21	-2.36	1.87
RE	EV assumed	0.13	146.00	0.89	0.26	1.97
	EV not assumed	0.13	144.94	0.89	0.26	1.95
AV	EV assumed	-1.91	146.00	0.06	-3.05	1.59
	EV not assumed	-1.94	139.06	0.05	-3.05	1.57
YL	EV assumed	-1.18	146.00	0.24	-2.39	2.03
	EV not assumed	-1.19	143.23	0.24	-2.39	2.01
HE	EV assumed	2.63	146.00	0.01	4.32	1.64
	EV not assumed	2.66	145.37	0.01	4.32	1.63
SC	EV assumed	-0.14	146.00	0.89	-0.19	1.33
	EV not assumed	-0.15	142.04	0.88	-0.19	1.31

In the case of the author's research, the T-Test was used to compare the means from Group 1 (the female group) and Group 2 (the male group). The T-test was an independent sample T-Test because the student respondents from the two groups were unrelated. Also, the level of significance was set at an alpha level of .05. This alpha level was set because the probability of a Type I error, in which the null hypothesis would be rejected, was 5%, or .05 (Frankfort-Nachmias & Leon-Guerrero, 2006, p. 412).

The T-tests for many behavioral responses were not significant, meaning that the responses were greater than the set level of significance, .05. For example, the conflict response of perspective taking, or PT, was listed at .296, which was greater than .05. Thus, the responses to PT were not significant. Therefore, the null hypothesis for gender could not be rejected. However, a few conflict responses, such as expressing emotions, EE (.000), reaching out (.005), reflective thinking, RO (.029), winning, WI (.007), and hiding emotions, HE (.009) were below the .05 level of significance (see Figure 7 and 8). This meant that the aforementioned behavioral responses were significant. Therefore, the null hypothesis can be rejected.

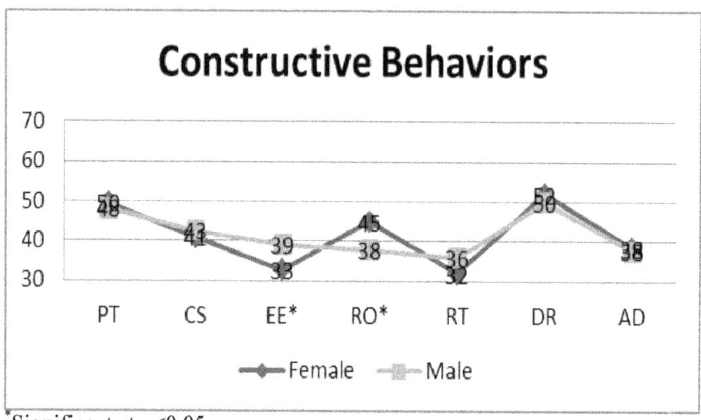

*Significant at p<0.05

Figure 7. Constructive behavioral responses for males and females.

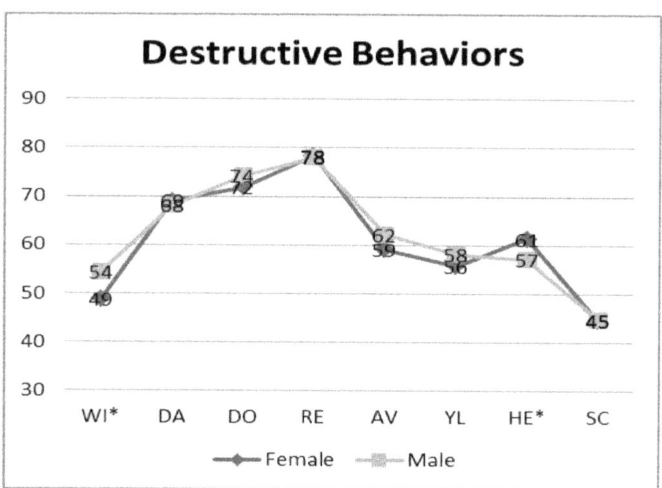

*Significant at p<0.05.

Figure 8. Destructive behavioral responses for males and females.

Table *8*

GENDER Group Statistics for Hot Button Responses

Group Statistics

	GENDER	N	Mean	Std. Deviation	Std. Error Mean
HBUNR	1	70	40.19	10.09	1.21
	2	78	37.17	11.66	1.32
HBOA	1	70	68.25	12.23	1.46
	2	78	61.28	11.97	1.36
HBUNA	1	70	55.55	11.27	1.35
	2	78	49.83	11.94	1.35
HBAL	1	70	56.00	9.90	1.18
	2	78	53.01	11.32	1.28
HBMI	1	70	52.79	9.62	1.15
	2	78	50.85	10.45	1.18
HBSE	1	70	52.95	9.23	1.10
	2	78	49.26	10.68	1.21
HBAB	1	70	46.18	9.43	1.13
	2	78	45.30	11.59	1.31
HBUNT	1	70	39.31	12.95	1.55
	2	78	33.46	13.08	1.48
HBHO	1	70	41.03	9.17	1.10
	2	78	39.51	9.74	1.10

Among all hot button responses, females were found to exhibit higher mean response scores than males. For example, females reported a higher mean response score than males in responding to unreliability, HBUNR. The mean response of females was 40.20, while the mean male response was 37.17. The higher mean scores in the female group, while below the set average score of 50, was also below the minimum threshold score of 45. However, females were found to be more upset at unreliable hot button behaviors than males. In addition, there was a greater variation in responses among men than among women. The standard deviation among males was 11.66, while for females it was 10.09. Both standard deviations were higher than the average standard deviation of 10, indicating large variations in responses in both gender groups. The standard error of the mean was also higher among males (1.32) than among females (1.21), indicating greater dispersion of scores around the mean. Thus, more females were likely to respond negativity to unreliable behaviors than males.

Table *9*

T-test for Gender Hot Buttons

Independent Samples Test

		t-test for Equality of Means			
		t	df	Sig. (2-tailed)	Mean Difference
HBUNR	EV assumed	1.68	146.00	0.10	3.02
	EV not assumed	1.69	145.82	0.09	3.02
HBOA	EV assumed	3.50	146.00	0.00	6.97
	EV not assumed	3.49	143.55	0.00	6.97
HBUNA	EV assumed	2.99	146.00	0.00	5.72
	EV not assumed	3.00	145.62	0.00	5.72
HBAL	EV assumed	1.70	146.00	0.09	2.99
	EV not assumed	1.71	145.91	0.09	2.99
HBMI	EV assumed	1.17	146.00	0.24	1.94
	EV not assumed	1.18	145.89	0.24	1.94
HBSE	EV assumed	2.24	146.00	0.03	3.70
	EV not assumed	2.26	145.81	0.03	3.70
HBAB	EV assumed	0.50	146.00	0.62	0.88
	EV not assumed	0.51	144.67	0.61	0.88
HBUNT	EV assumed	2.73	146.00	0.01	5.84
	EV not assumed	2.73	144.59	0.01	5.84
HBHO	EV assumed	0.98	146.00	0.33	1.53
	EV not assumed	0.98	145.66	0.33	1.53

The T-Test was used to compare the means from Group 1 (the female group) and Group 2 (the male group). According to Table 9, several hot button responses were significant for gender. For example, significant responses included over-analytical, HBOA (.001), unappreciative, HBUNA (.003), self-centered, HBSE (.027), and untrustworthy, HBUNT (.007). The responses were lower than the set level of significance of .05, meaning that gender was a significant factor in responses to hot button behaviors (see Figure 9). Thus, the null hypothesis for gender may be rejected based on the results of these particular conflict responses.

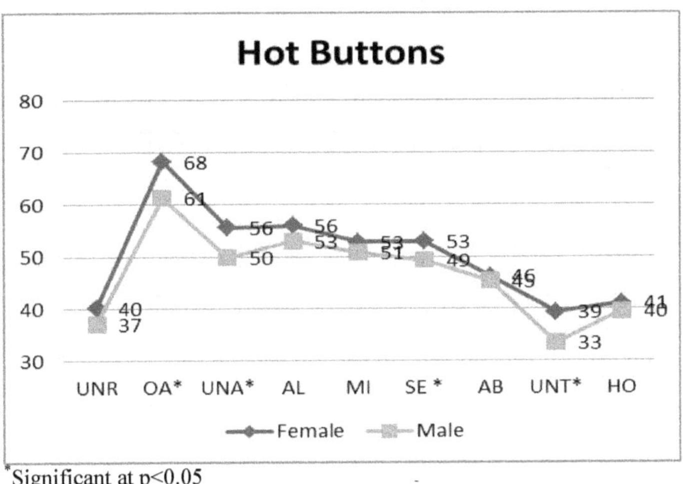

*Significant at p<0.05

Figure 9. Hot buttons for males and females.

Income

<u>H4:   Students of different socioeconomic backgrounds will have different responses to CDP scale scores.</u>

Table *10*

One-way ANOVA for Income and Constructive and Destructive Responses to Conflict

ANOVA

		Sum of Squares	df	Mean Square	F	Sig.
PT	Between Groups	43.21	3.00	14.40	0.23	0.88
	Within Groups	9134.03	146.00	62.56		
	Total	9177.24	149.00			
CS	Between Groups	102.12	3.00	34.04	0.31	0.82
	Within Groups	16046.56	146.00	109.91		
	Total	16148.68	149.00			
EE	Between Groups	83.13	3.00	27.71	0.33	0.80
	Within Groups	12220.96	146.00	83.71		
	Total	12304.09	149.00			
RO	Between Groups	338.64	3.00	112.88	0.48	0.69
	Within Groups	34048.72	146.00	233.21		
	Total	34387.36	149.00			
RT	Between Groups	599.49	3.00	199.83	1.62	0.19
	Within Groups	18062.63	146.00	123.72		
	Total	18662.12	149.00			
DR	Between Groups	115.50	3.00	38.50	0.23	0.88
	Within Groups	24957.57	146.00	170.94		
	Total	25073.07	149.00			
AD	Between Groups	131.79	3.00	43.93	0.21	0.89
	Within Groups	30320.19	146.00	207.67		
	Total	30451.98	149.00			
WI	Between Groups	285.79	3.00	95.26	0.60	0.62
	Within Groups	23275.93	146.00	159.42		
	Total	23561.71	149.00			
DA	Between Groups	145.67	3.00	48.56	0.48	0.70
	Within Groups	14743.87	146.00	100.99		
	Total	14889.54	149.00			
DO	Between Groups	51.57	3.00	17.19	0.13	0.94
	Within Groups	19714.35	146.00	135.03		
	Total	19765.91	149.00			

		Sum of Squares	df	Mean Square	F	Sig.
RE	Between Groups	332.92	3.00	110.97	0.79	0.50
	Within Groups	20603.51	146.00	141.12		
	Total	20936.43	149.00			
AV	Between Groups	211.20	3.00	70.40	0.74	0.53
	Within Groups	13912.76	146.00	95.29		
	Total	14123.95	149.00			
YL	Between Groups	441.61	3.00	147.20	0.98	0.41
	Within Groups	22046.21	146.00	151.00		
	Total	22487.81	149.00			
HE	Between Groups	87.78	3.00	29.26	0.28	0.84
	Within Groups	15187.26	146.00	104.02		
	Total	15275.04	149.00			
SC	Between Groups	20.92	3.00	6.97	0.11	0.96
	Within Groups	9530.48	146.00	65.28		
	Total	9551.40	149.00			

The one-way ANOVA analysis results indicated that for all 15 behavioral responses, the probabilities were higher than the set .05 level of significance. Therefore, income is not a significant factor in how the surveyed students respond to conflicts. As such, the null hypothesis for income was not rejected.

Table *11*

One-way ANOVA for INCOME and Hot Button Responses

ANOVA

		Sum of Squares	df	Mean Square	F	Sig.
HBUNR	Between Groups	323.42	3.00	107.81	0.89	0.45
	Within Groups	17764.45	146.00	121.67		
	Total	18087.87	149.00			
HBOA	Between Groups	628.68	3.00	209.56	1.36	0.26
	Within Groups	22541.14	146.00	154.39		
	Total	23169.83	149.00			
HBUNA	Between Groups	776.37	3.00	258.79	1.86	0.14
	Within Groups	20266.71	146.00	138.81		
	Total	21043.08	149.00			

HBAL	Between Groups	235.02	3.00	78.34	0.67	0.57
	Within Groups	16996.13	146.00	116.41		
	Total	17231.15	149.00			
HBMI	Between Groups	85.73	3.00	28.58	0.28	0.84
	Within Groups	14983.58	146.00	102.63		
	Total	15069.31	149.00			
HBSE	Between Groups	109.14	3.00	36.38	0.35	0.79
	Within Groups	15278.31	146.00	104.65		
	Total	15387.45	149.00			
HBAB	Between Groups	156.86	3.00	52.29	0.47	0.71
	Within Groups	16378.11	146.00	112.18		
	Total	16534.97	149.00			
HBUNT	Between Groups	232.56	3.00	77.52	0.43	0.73
	Within Groups	26441.78	146.00	181.11		
	Total	26674.34	149.00			
HBHO	Between Groups	161.46	3.00	53.82	0.60	0.62
	Within Groups	13208.94	146.00	90.47		
	Total	13370.40	149.00			

The results indicated that there were no significant differences between incomes in terms of responses to hot button behaviors. All of the probabilities were greater than the set .05 level of significance. Thus, the income of the respondent has no effect on responses to hot button behaviors, and the null hypothesis for income cannot be rejected.

Chapter 5: Discussion and Implications of the Study

Introduction

The research explored the effects of social factors on responses to conflicts among community college students. The researcher measured the independent variables of age, ethnicity, gender, and socioeconomic background on the dependent variable, responses to conflicts, using the Conflict Dynamic Profile-Individual (CDP-I) instrument. Using the CDP-I, the author examined how students of various ages, ethnicities, genders, and socioeconomic backgrounds respond to conflicts in active-constructive, passive-constructive, active-destructive, and passive-destructive manners. The author also measured hot button responses to conflict based on the students' social factors. The researcher conducted an online survey of 150 community college students through Zoomerang, in which they answered the CDP-I Questionnaire. The responses were analyzed using SPSS version 19, t-test, and one-way ANOVA. It was found that gender was a significant social factor in how community college students respond to conflicts. The other independent variables of age, ethnicity, and socioeconomic background were not significant factors in responses to conflict.

Discussion

The author decided to research the topic due to his background in community colleges. The author taught a total of 10 years at the community college level, gaining experience with diverse groups of students. He was intrigued by how these groups can function cohesively, despite their differences. The author was also interested in what causes students to disagree with each other and how their background influences their reaction to conflict situations. When researching the topic, the author found information on community college performance among students, teachers, and even school systems, but not on conflict resolution. Also, he realized that from personal experience, conflicts were handled in a bureaucratic fashion by the Dean of Students, often resulting in dismissal from the school or suspension for the semester. As a result, the author wanted to find a method of dealing with conflicts through mediation, as opposed to administratively punitive sanctions. Thus, by examining the responses of different demographic groups to conflict, a community college may institute mediation programs that address those differences. One example is peer mediation. If conflict arises on campus, then a group of peer mediators, along with the Dean of Students, may intercede to offer solutions to the conflicts. Such solutions may be manifested in a verbal or written agreement. However, if the conflict or its response is extreme, resulting in bodily injury or great emotional or psychological harm, then mediation may not be appropriate. Instead, extreme matters should be addressed by the Dean of Students, the college president, and/or law enforcement authorities.

Hypotheses

The variables examined were age, ethnicity, gender, and socioeconomic background because they represented broader demographics within the community college system. For instance, there are younger, as well as older students at community college campuses. Likewise, there are different ethnic groups represented on campus, along with different genders and students from various income levels. Age was selected as an independent variable because of the large numbers of students who are over the age of 20 on campus. As mentioned in the introduction, the average age of a community college was 28 (American Association of Community Colleges, 2011). Since there are diverse ages of students in a given community college classroom, the author wanted to ascertain any differences in how younger students handle conflict, versus older students. The first hypothesis, H1, stated that students of different ages will have different responses to conflicts on community college campuses. The results did not reflect that hypothesis. In fact, none of the conflict responses were found to be statistically significant. Thus, age was found not to be a social factor in how students respond to conflicts. A possible reason for the high response rates of younger students could be that this demographic group, which ranges from 18-24 years of age, was born during the dawn of the Internet age, which began in the early 1990s. As a result, younger students of this age cohort attended primary and secondary schools equipped with computers that accessed the Internet. This 'Internet-savvy' group was also exposed to online tests and surveys at an early age. Thus, many were able to access Zoomerang with relative ease. The older students, on the other hand, received exposure to the Internet at a relatively later stage, perhaps in the workplace, or as adult students. Thus, many older students were probably not familiar with the Zoomerang service.

Ethnicity was another interesting independent variable that was chosen by the author. As of 2011, 45% of community college students were ethnic minorities (American Association of Community Colleges, 2011). Since such a large percentage of community college students are minorities, the author expected diverse responses to conflict based on ethnicity. However, the results proved otherwise. There was no significant difference in how different ethnic groups responded to conflicts. A possible reason for the results could be that many minorities have been assimilated into mainstream American society and adopted its cultural norms, which may include responses to conflicts.

The only hypothesis in which the responses to conflict were statistically significant was the third hypothesis, H3, which stated that students of different genders will have different responses to conflicts on community college campuses. Gender was chosen because of the growing number of women on community college campuses. In fact, 58% of community college students are female (American Association of Community Colleges, 2011). Statistically significant scores were found in the active-constructive responses of expressing emotions (EE) and reaching out (RE), the passive-constructive response of reflective thinking (RT), the active-destructive response of winning (WI), and the passive-destructive response of hiding emotions (HE). In addition, statistically significant scores were found in the hot button responses of over-analytical (HBOA), unappreciative (HBUNA), self-centered (HBSE), and untrustworthy (HBUNT).

For the active-constructive response of expressing emotions (EE), the T-test indicated a significance of .000, which is highly significant for gender because that score is below the alpha level of .05. This significance means that there is a difference in how males and females express emotions. The mean response for females was 33, while for males it was 39. Both mean responses were below the average response score of 50. However, males scored higher on expressing emotions than females, which means that males expressed more emotions than females. The author did not expect that males would express emotions more than females, especially since previous research, such as Sax and Harper (2007), reported that females were more likely to express emotions than males.

Also, in the active-constructive response, reaching out (RE), the significance was .01, which was lower than the set alpha level of .05. Males and females reported different mean responses in this category. In fact, females reported a mean response score of 45, while males reported a mean response score of 38. Both scores were below the average response score of 50. However, it can be inferred that females were more likely to reach out than males when responding to conflict. These results were expected, correlating with research from previous academics such as Sax and Harper (2007).

In the passive-constructive response of reflective thinking (RT), the differences between the genders were significant at .03, which was lower than the set level of significance of .05. When examining the difference in mean responses, females scored a lower mean (32) response than males (36). Even though both responses were below the average score of 50, males were more likely than females to engage in reflective thinking. The author expected the opposite trend to occur, which was that females were more likely to be engaged in reflective thinking.

For the active-destructive response of winning (WI), the significance was .01, which was lower than the set level of significance of .05. According to the results, males were found to have a higher mean response (54) than females (49). Both response scores were at or slightly above the set average score of 50, meaning that both genders scored high on winning. However, the fact that males scored higher than females signifies that males were more likely than females to display attitudes of winning. These results were what the author expected because previous researchers found males to display higher levels of aggressiveness than females.

The passive-destructive response of hiding emotions (HE) indicated a significance of .01, which was lower than the set level of significance of .05, meaning that there were gender differences in how participants hid emotions. The results indicated that females displayed a higher mean response (61) than males (57). This meant that females were more likely to hide emotions than males. The findings were surprising to the author because it contradicted past research that suggested women were more likely to display emotions than men.

In addition, statistically significant scores were found in the hot button responses of over-analytical (HBOA), unappreciative (HBUNA), self-centered (HBSE), and untrustworthy (HBUNT). In the over-analytical category, the significance was .000, indicating significant gender differences in how people respond to over-analytical behavior. Females were found to have a higher response mean (68) than males (61). Both responses were higher than the average set score of 50, meaning that both genders reacted negatively to over-analytical behavior. Thus, females were more likely than males to respond negatively to over-analytical behavior. The author expected that females would display more negative responses to the behavior than men because such reaction may indicate anxiety, which was found by Sax and Harper (2007) to be higher in college-aged women than among men.

Unappreciative behavioral responses were found to be statistically significant at .000, indicating differences between the genders. Females exhibited higher mean responses (56) than males (50). Both genders responded at or above the set average mean score of 50, indicating that they reacted rather negatively to the behavior. Females were more likely than males to respond negatively to unappreciative behavior. The findings were what the author expected because past studies indicated that females were found by past researchers to volunteer better than males.

In the hot button behavior of self-centered, the significance was .03, meaning that there were differences between the genders in responses to the behavior. Females exhibited a higher response score (53) than males (49). Both scores were at or above the set average of 50, indicating that both genders reacted negatively to self-centered behavior. The results were congruent with past research by Sax and Harper (2007) that found females were more likely to be engaged in social activism than males, which requires persons to care about others, rather than become self-centered individuals.

Untrustworthy behavioral responses were found to have a significance of .01, which meant that males and females reacted differently to untrustworthy individuals. Females displayed a higher mean response (39) than males (33). Both scores were below average, which meant that the responses were not very negative. However, the fact that females were more likely to respond negatively than males to untrustworthy behaviors confirmed Sax and Harper's (2007) findings that females were more likely to become involved in social activism in college. Social activism may require a great deal of trust in order for success to occur.

Finally, the author chose socioeconomic background as an independent variable because community colleges are open institutions in terms of income. Many community college students are not from economical privileged families. On the contrary, 59% of community college students are employed part-time, and 59% of students are on financial aid. Thus, community colleges are attractive to students of limited financial means. The fourth hypothesis, H4, stated that students of different socioeconomic backgrounds will have different responses to conflicts on community college campuses. The results of the research indicated that there were no significant differences in income when it came to responses to conflict. The results could be indicative of higher numbers of middle-income students entering community colleges. The recent trend could be the result of the rising costs of four-year colleges and universities, coupled with the economic troubles associated with Great Recession.

Implications of the Study

The research has several implications for conflict resolution at the community college level. One implication is in the area of gender studies. The findings of the research demonstrated that more males than females were likely to engage in reflective thinking and winning. On the other hand, more females than males were likely to respond to conflicts by reaching out and hiding emotions. The results may signify that gender roles have rapidly changed and that females have the same career and educational opportunities. At the same time, both genders are exposed to high levels of daily stress. It could be said that females are exhibiting behavioral responses to conflicts in similar ways to their male counterparts. This pattern of behavior could mean that both genders may need increased conflict resolution training in how to respond to conflicts in a constructive manner. The training can be performed at work, at the community college, or through relationship therapy. Since gender was seen as a significant factor in how community college students respond to conflicts, further research into gender differences is warranted.

Several community colleges, as well as four-year colleges, utilize conflict resolution workshops aimed at gender issues. At Portland Community College in Portland, Oregon, a gender conflict resolution course is aimed at addressing gender and conflict resolution (Portland Community College Class Schedule, 2012). The one credit hour online course, which lasts for five weeks, gives students an opportunity to interact with others through individual research and group discussions. Each student is asked about their gender culture, as well exploring multicultural communication. In addition, students learn to identify sources of conflict, as well as strategies for managing conflicts (Portland Community College Class Schedule, 2012). Students gather research materials through the college library. As for grades, students are evaluated on the quality of research, participation in discussions, and the thought placed into the activities (Portland Community College Class Schedule, 2012).

Another implication of the research is in how administrators address conflicts among diverse groups of students on community college campuses. Not every conflict at a community college campus should result in suspension or expulsion. Some conflicts may be referred to a campus mediator. Those mediators, in turn, may be trained in how to manage conflicts. Also, peer mediators can be trained every semester to assist administrators in resolving conflicts. The reason for the semester training is to ensure that enough mediators are available for students. This is important given the high transfer rate of students at community colleges, as well as the part-time status of many students. The peer mediator will be available for cases such as classroom or parking lot disputes. As long as the disputes are not criminal in nature, the student mediators would be able to address the case. Training of peer mediators should be under the auspices of the Dean of Students of the community college. The dean may use a trained faculty member or administrator for conflict resolution training. If that is not feasible, then the dean may hire an external conflict resolution trainer to facilitate the training of the peer mediators and administrators. The mediators should always report their findings to the dean. If the case cannot be solved through the mediators, then the Dean of Students is the final arbiter. In short, greater study of community college mediation techniques should continue in order for mediation to become a common option on campus.

An example of college mediation programs is Dickinson College's Conflict Resolution Resource Center. Located in Carlisle, PA, the center offers several services, including coaching sessions and mediation to students and faculty members. In addition, the center operates a program called 'Sustained Dialogue at Dickinson'. Furthermore, the Conflict Resolution Resource Center created a collection of books that are available at Dickinson College's library (Dickinson College Conflict Resolution Resource Center, 2012).

An integral part of the Conflict Resolution Resource Center is the mediation program. Mediation services that are offered at Dickinson College are voluntary. However, conflicting parties are encouraged to attend these services by authority figures. Mediation services at the college are also confidential, and that the only information released to authority figures would be confirmation that the parties attended mediation and whether or not an agreement was reached by the parties (Dickinson College-Mediation, 2012). At Dickinson College, students, faculty, staff, and administrators take advantage of mediation programs. In terms of students, mediation is used to settle roommate disputes that could not be resolved by the parties or residential assistants (RAs), intra-group conflicts involving student clubs, student/advisors, inter and intra-fraternity conflicts, student/faculty and student/staff conflicts, and parking issues (Dickinson College-Mediation, 2012). Student mediation is conducted using peer mediators, who report to the Assistant Provost. The Assistant Provost is also the director of the Conflict Resolution Resources Center (Dickinson College-Mediation, 2012).

A further implication of the author's research is in the area of community college student development. While the other two implications of inter-gender and mediation training are of great concern, college retention and development is an equally important concern. Conflict, if unchecked, may undermine the role of community colleges in providing a cost-effective, quality education. Simply put, out-of-control conflict situations and ineffective responses may drive students elsewhere, thus ruining the reputation of the community college. As a result, high-performing students and different social groups may transfer in large numbers, thus resulting in decreased diversity on campus, and thus reducing the educational and social quality of the college. For example, the author discussed previous research regarding Allport's Contact Theory, which was mentioned by Maxwell and Shammas (2007). Allport's Contact Theory posits that contact between different groups of college students tend to decrease the amount of prejudice (Maxwell & Shammas, 2007, pp. 345-346). The lessening of prejudice is based on communication and common values (p. 346). The reduction of conflict has to do, in part, with understanding common values and effective communication. Community colleges may wish to institute workshops aimed at lessening harmful stereotypes and fostering greater cooperation. These workshops may be held once a semester and can be aimed at incoming freshmen. Also, the workshops may be held in conjunction with the peer mediation program, so that students can become aware of the resources available to them. Thus, the dissertation study may serve as a beginning point for research into understanding how community college students may help improve the quality of campus life.

An example of workshops aimed at promoting exposure to diverse groups would be those operated by the Office of Intercultural Affairs at Stonehill College (Easton, Massachusetts). This office contains workshop resources such as film discussions, professional training, and class-specific presentations. For example, practitioners in the department use class-specific presentations in education and teacher training. During these workshops, participants are taught ways in which intercultural awareness can be increased. Also, participants are taught reflective exercises designed for teachers to gain insight into what they bring to the classroom (Stonehill College-Intercultural Affairs, 2012).

Another example of workshops that bring awareness to diversity was described by Jeanne Helm (2000), when she discussed a diversity sensitivity workshop that helped change students her a junior college classroom (Helms, 2000, p. 63). In the article, Helm described how a college counselor, Marcus, conducted a diversity workshop to Helm's child care classroom consisting of 25 students who were reading a section on diversity. Marcus began the program by introducing the class to a workshop concept called 'barnga,' which is a belief that all people have similarities and differences (Helm, 2000, p. 63). Part of barnga included participation in a card game called spades amd students were required to 'read the rules.' During this exercise, students could not talk, but Helm noticed that the students may have uncomfortable thoughts about the card game and each other (Helm, 2000, p. 63).

At the conclusion of the exercise, students were asked by Marcus to reveal their thoughts. The students exchanged a variety of thoughts and emotions (Helm, 2000, p. 63). Inspired by Marcus, Helm developed 12 techniques that may help students understand bias. Those steps included; 1) chart presentations, in which students were split into groups of three in order to present a chart that discussed family fears and barriers to language, 2) development of a community survey, in which students interview child care directors and parents to assess family traditions, 3) the making of quilts in the classroom to illustrate each person's culture, 4) the use of PowerPoint and slides by students to report their approaches to diversity, 5) a director's forum, in which surveys are given to local child care center directors. The results are then shared with Helm's class as a presentation, 6) creating 'what would you do if' cards for scenarios aimed at problem-solving, 7) using board games to address sticky situations involving diversity, 8) journal-keeping by students, meant ro serve as a confidential dialogue between the student and the instructor, 9) the use of verbal dialogues between students, which may be passionate but respectful, 10) process dramas, in which students enact role plays meant to create problem solving skills, 11) writing comments on an easel, where students post comments during breaks, and finally, 12) the grouping of students into pairs in order to play a game called 'are we similar?' In this activity, student pairs are given scissors, glue, markers, and clay and are asked to write down similar events in their lives (pp. 64-65).

The 12-step activities that are promoted by Helm may be used in any community college setting. These activities may be used with the assistance of peer mediators, instructors, and staff members. The author suggests that Helm's activities be utilized at all community colleges. However, the workshops seem very flexible and may be adapted for use according to the regional culture of the community.

Further Implications

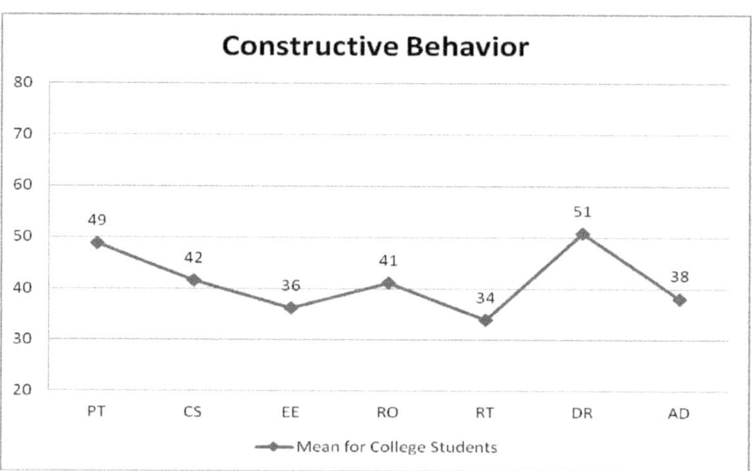

Figure 10. Constructive behavioral responses for all groups.

Some of the constructive responses to conflict were below average. For instance, the lowest mean score was expressing emotions. To address this issue, community colleges should hold workshops for all students, regardless of demographic background, on the importance of expressing appropriate emotions.

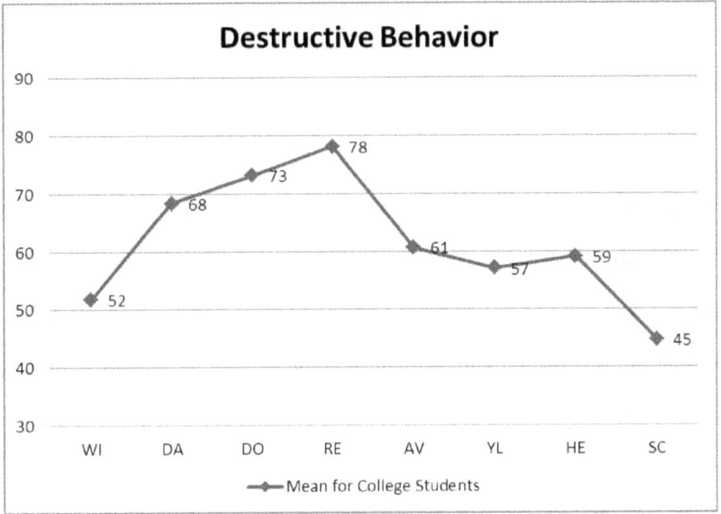

Figure 11. Destructive responses for all groups.

With the exception of self-criticizing, all of the destructive responses were at or above the set average response of 50. This indicates that most community college students need to better respond to conflicts. Workshops held at the beginning of the semester may be needed to prevent incoming students from undertaking responses that could result in negative consequences, such as expulsion from the college.

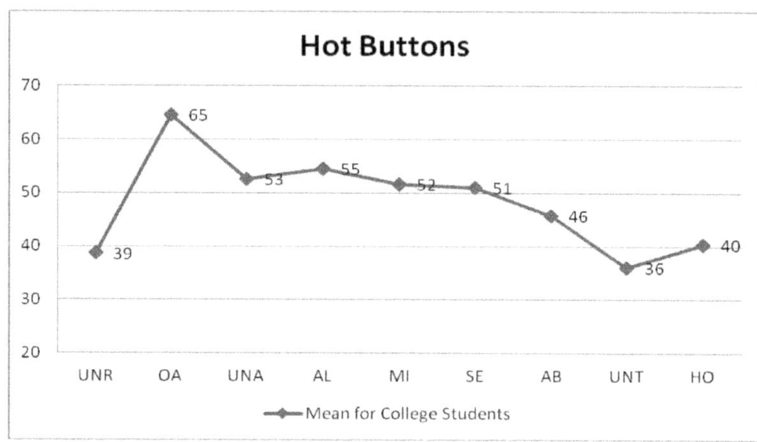

Figure 12. Hot button responses for all groups.

In terms of hot button responses, all groups reported higher than average responses to many hot button behaviors. This is especially true when students responded to over-analytical people. Seminars and other training sessions are needed to assist community college students address people displaying hot button behaviors. Like destructive responses, hot button behaviors can potentially increase the likelihood of destructive conflict. At a community college, these responses may result in physical altercations or shouting matches. Reducing negative responses to hot button behaviors will assist in developing conflict resolution skills that can be applied to the workplace.

Contribution of the Research

The research may be beneficial to the field of conflict resolution in two important ways. First, genders may be better able to communicate with each other during and after conflicts. For instance, the results indicated that more males than females were likely to engage in reflective thinking and winning. On the other hand, more females than males were likely to respond to conflicts by reaching out and hiding emotions. The findings may be applied to gender relationship workshops, where women who were emotionally hurt by interpersonal conflict may be taught how to be more assertive and to better express their feelings. Workshop participants may be given the CDP-I as a pre-test to determine their responses. If females scored low on reflective thinking or scored high on hiding emotions, then the workshop may gear its focus towards developing skills in assertiveness and positive emotional expression. At the conclusion of the workshop, the same participants may be given a post-test CDP-I to measure areas of improvement. If the females showed improved response scores in the areas of reflective thinking or hiding emotions, then the workshop would have been effective in its goal of improving communication skills among females. These improved skills may give females with relationship issues the ability to better negotiate problems that can arise, for example, in marriages, friendships, or domestic partnerships.

Second, the author's research could be applicable in the area of peer mediation. The findings in the hot button issues of unappreciative responses showed that females exhibited a higher mean response than males. In other words, females were more likely to respond negatively to people displaying unappreciative behaviors than males. The result of these responses can be manifested in the classroom, where arguments could break out between males and females. If that were to occur, students may be referred to peer mediators, who can assist in helping each gender understand how the opposite sex communicates. It is not always what is said that is contentious, but how it is said, and how the opposite sex interprets it. Some males, for instance, may want to share something of value with females whilst in the midst of a discussion in class, but end up putting their proverbial 'foot in their mouth.' Peer mediators can help males avoid that faux pas by explaining how females may interpret certain things. That task is not easy to do, and some colloquial words may differ by geographical region, but in most societies, mediators are able to distinguish what can be appropriately shared between genders.

Strengths and Limitations of the Study

The research conducted by the author has several strengths as well as its limitations. As for strengths, the research explored a little-understood aspect of community college culture, which was the study of conflict. Much of the literature concerning community colleges focused on transfer rates and achievement levels among different social groups of students. However, little is known about the interaction between these groups of students on campus. The results of this research may be the impetus towards further study of student behavioral interaction at community colleges. Another strength of this research was the use of Zoomerang as a survey tool. The service was able to distribute surveys throughout the entire country. Zoomerang saved the author much needed time because distributing the surveys would have involved seeking approval from multiple community college sites. With Zoomerang, the community college students were already identified from previous studies.

As with every research study, there are limitations that are present. One limitation faced by the author was the number of respondents. Due to the limited budget of the author, 150 respondents were selected. It could be speculated that the demographic results may have been different, especially in the age category where 87% of respondents were reported to be in the 18-24 age group. Perhaps future studies could use 200 or more respondents, yielding a more diverse group of respondents. Also, the study could have expanded the number of independent variables to include rural versus urban students, freshmen versus sophomore students, and students who live at home with parents. The author believes that the results would reflect greater differences between students based on these additional variables.

The author would recommend the use of the study to further develop gender research by explaining why males and females respond to conflicts differently. The author's study found that differences did indeed exist in constructive, destructive, and hot button responses. However, the study did not ascertain the reason(s) why the responses differed by gender. Future studies can even examine gender differences to conflict responses according to ethnicity and class. These topics are of great interest to sociologists, psychologists, and marriage therapists because both genders may better understand why responses to conflicts could lead to divorces.

Another future research concept is violence prevention. Recent school shootings on high school and college campus highlight the need for students to develop skills that can assist them in responding appropriately to conflict. Among the many conflict responses, the author examined hot button responses, in which people respond to hot buttons, or irritable behaviors. The research can be utilized to help counselors at community colleges identify students who score high on hot button responses and destructive responses and refer them to therapy. The sooner that students can be taught how beneficial conflict resolution skills such as cooperation and creating win-win solutions are, the better equipped they are to properly respond to conflicts. Properly trained community college students may even teach their classmates how to respond to hot buttons in constructive ways, thereby reducing the likelihood of violence.

Summary

Conflict resolution is an exciting field in which a broad range of issues can be addressed. The research study that was conducted addressed the use of conflict resolution in post-secondary education, more specifically, community college settings. Since community colleges are open institutions, attracting a wide swath of American society, there is bound to be conflict. The author's research attempted to understand demographic differences in responses to conflicts at the community college level. The results indicated that major differences in gender exist in terms of responses to conflict. Based on those findings, further study needs to be conducted to understand how males and females can better communicate with each other. In addition, more research should occur in community colleges to ascertain the needs of a rapidly growing and socially diverse student population so that these individuals can be successful in their chosen careers.

References

American Association of Community Colleges. (2011). 2011 Fact Sheet. Retrieved from http://www.aacc.nche.edu/AboutCC/Documents/FactSheet2011.pdf

Bailey, T., Calcagno, J. C., Jenkins, D., Leinbach, T., & Kienzl, G. (2006). Is the student right-to-know all you should know? An analysis of community college graduation rates. *Research in Higher Education, 47*(5), 491-519. Retrieved from http://www.jstor.org/stable/40197600

Baum, S., Payea, K., & Steele, P. (2006). *Education pays: Second update-A supplement to education pays 2004: The benefits of higher education for individuals and society.* Retrieved from http://www.eaop.org/documents/college _board_edu_pays_update_ 2006.pdf

Beebe, S., Mottet, T., & Roach, K. (2004). *Training and development: Enhancing communication and leadership skills.* Boston: Pearson Education, Inc.

Calcagno, J., Crosta, P., Bailey, T., & Jenkins, D. (2007). Does age of entrant affect community college completion rates: Evidence from a discrete-time hazard model. *Educational Evaluation and Policy Analysis, 29*(3), 218-235. Retrieved from http://www.jstor.org/stable/30128031

Capobianco, S., Davis, M., & Kraus, L. (2008a). *Facilitator guide: Conflict dynamic profile individual* (pp. 1-6). St. Petersburg, FL: Center for Conflict Dynamics at Eckerd College.

Capobianco, S., Davis, M., & Kraus, L. (2008b). *Conflict dynamic profile technical guide* (pp. 1-6). St. Petersburg, FL: Center for Conflict Dynamics at Eckerd College.

Capobianco, S., Davis, M., & Kraus, L. (2008c). *Conflict dynamic profile individual version Feedback report* (pp. 1-8). St. Petersburg, FL: Center for Conflict Dynamics at Eckerd College.

Capobianco, S., Davis, M., & Kraus, L. (2008d). *Conflict dynamic profile: Feedback report* (p. 5). St. Petersburg, FL: Center for Conflict Dynamics at Eckerd College.

Capobianco, S., Davis, M., & Kraus, L. (2009). *Conflict dynamic profile: Development guide*. St. Petersburg, FL: Center for Conflict Dynamics at Eckerd College.

Chang, J. (2005). Faculty-student interaction at the community college: A focus on students of color. *Research in Higher Education, 46*(7), 769-802. Retrieved from http://www.jstor.org/stable/40197445

Cheung. C., & Chan, K. (2010). Social capital as exchange: Its contribution to morale. *Social Indicators Research, 96*(2), 205-227. doi:10.1007/s11205-009-9570-2

CNN.com. (2010). *Community colleges are focus of White House summit*. Retrieved from http://m.cnn.com/primary/_IcR8oR-isVMriFN2X

Cohen, A., & Brawer, F. (1996). *The American community college* (3rd ed.). San Francisco: Jossey-Bass.

Conflict Dynamic Profile. (2011). *CDP online assessment instructors for certified users*. St. Petersburg, FL: Center for Conflict Dynamics at Eckerd College.

Corenblum, B., & Stephan, W. (2001). White fears and native apprehensions: An integrated threat approach to intergroup attitudes. *Canadian Journal of Behavioural Science, 33*(4), 251-268. doi:10.1037/h0087147

Creswell, J. (1998). *Qualitative inquiry and research design: Choosing among five traditions.* Thousand Oaks, CA: Sage Publications.

Darkenwald, Jr., G. (1971). Organizational conflict in colleges and universities. *Administrative Sciences Quarterly, 16*(4), 407-412. Retrieved from http://www.jstor.org/stable/2391761

Davidson, J., & Wood, C. (2004). A conflict resolution model. *Theory Into Practice, 43*(1), 6-13. Retrieved from http://www.jstor.org/stable/3701559

Dee, J., Henkin, A., & Holman, F. (2004). Reconciling differences: Conflict management strategies of catholic college and university presidents. *Higher Education, 47*(2), 177-196. Retrieved from http://www.jstor.org/stable/4151538

Dickinson College. (2012). Dickinson College: Conflict Resolution Resource Center. Retrieved from http://dickinson.edu/academics/resources/conflict-resolution-resource-center/

Dickinson College. (2012). Dickinson: Mediation. Retrieved from http://dickinson.edu/academics/resources/conflict-resolution-resource-center/content/Mediation/

Dougherty, K. (1994). *The contradictory college: The conflicting origins, impacts, and futures of the community college.* Albany, NY: State University of New York Press.

Dowd, A. (2003). From access to outcome equity: Revitalizing the democratic mission of the community college. *Annals of the American Academy of Political and Social Sciences, 586,* 92-119. Retrieved from http://www.jstor.org/stable/1049722

Dowd, A., & Coury, T. (2006). The effect of loans on the persistence and attainment of community college students. *Research in Higher Education, 47*(1), 33-62. Retrieved from http://www.jstor.org/stable/40185883

Eckerd College. (2009). *Conflict dynamic profile individual questionnaire* (pp.1-4). St. Petersburg, FL: Center for Conflict Dynamics at Eckerd College.

Frankfort-Nachmias, C., & Leon-Guerrero, A. (2006). *Social statistics for adverse society* (4th ed.). Thousand Oaks, CA: Pine Forge Press.

Gill, A., & Leigh, D. (2000). Community college enrollment, college major, and the gender gap. *Industrial and Labor Relations Review, 54*(1), 163-181. Retrieved from http://www.jstor.org/stable/2696037

Haveman, R., & Smeeding, T. (2006). The role of higher education in social mobility. *The Future of Children, 16*(2), 125-150. Retrieved from http:jstor.org/stable/3844794

Helm, J. (2000). Marcus did it: A review of a diversity workshop and other creative education practices for college classrooms. Retrieved from ceep.crc.uiuc.edu/pubs/katzsym/helm.pdf

Jacoby, D. (2006). Effects of part-time faculty employment on community college graduation rates. *The Journal of Higher Education, 77*(6), 1081-1103. Retrieved from http:www.jstor.org/stable/4122368

Kim, D., Twombly, S., & Wolf-Wendel, L. (2008). Factors predicting community college faculty satisfaction with instructional autonomy. *Community College Review, 35*(3), 159-180.

Kriesberg, L. (2003). *Constructive conflicts: From escalation to resolution.* (2nd Ed). Lanham, MD: Rowman and Littlefield Publishers, Inc.

Lawler, E. J., Thye, S. R., & Yoon, J. (2008). Social exchange and micro social order. *American Sociological Association Review, 73*(4), 519-542. Retrieved from http://www.jstor.org/stable/25472543

Lee, V., & Frank, K. (1990). Students' characteristics that facilitate the transfer from two-year to four-year colleges. *Sociology of Education, 63*(3), 178-193. Retrieved from http://www.jstor.org/stable/2112836

Maxwell, W., Hagedorn, L. S., Cypers, S., Moon, H. S., Brocato, P., Wahl, K., & Prather, G. (2003). Community and diversity in urban community colleges: Coursetaking among entering students. *Community College Review, 30*(4), 21-46.

Maxwell, W., & Shammas, D. (2007). Research on race and ethnic relations among community college students. *Community College Review, 34*(4), 344-361.

Mellow, G., & Heelan, C. (2008). *Minding the dream: The Process and practice of the American community college.* Lanham, MD: Bowman and Littlefield.

Molm, L., Collett, J., & Shaefer, D. (2006). Conflict and fairness in social exchange. *Social Forces, 84*(4), 2331-2352. Retrieved from http://www.jstor.org/stable/3844503

Moore, C. (2003). *The mediation process: Practical strategies for resolving conflict.* San Francisco: Jossey-Bass.

National Center for Educational Statistics. (2011). *2008-2009 Baccalaureate and beyond longitudinal study.*Retrieved from

http://nces.ed.gov/pubsearch/pubsinfo.asp?pubid=2011236

Palazesi, L., & Bower, B. (2006). Self-identification modification and intent to return: Baby boomers reinvent themselves using the community college. *Community College Review, 34*(1), 44-67. doi:10.1177/0091552106289763

Portland Community College. (2012). Class schedule: MSD110 Gender conflict resolution. Retrieved from http://www.pcc.edu/schedule/default.cfm ?fa=dspCourse2&thisTerm=201203&crsCode=MSD110&subjCode=MSD&crsN um=110&topicCode=MSD&subtopicCode=

Radcliff, J. (1986). Should we forget William Rainey Harper? *Community College Review, 13*(4), 12-19. doi:10.1177/009155218601300403

Radcliff, J. (2009). *Community colleges: The history of community colleges, The junior college and the research university: The community college mission.* Retrieved from education.stateuniversity.com/pages/1873/Community-Colleges.html

Sax, L., & Harper, C. (2007). Origins of the gender gap: Pre-college and college influences on differences between men and women. *Research in Higher Education, 48*(6), 669-694. doi:10.1007/s11162-006-9046-z

Scoggin, D., & Styron, R. (2006). Factors associated with student withdrawal from community colleges. *Community College Enterprises, 12*(1), 111-124.

Seelman, K. L., & Walls, N. E. (2010). Person-organization incongruence as a predictor

of right-wing authoritarianism, social dominance orientation, and heterosexism.

Journal of Social Work Education, 46(1), 103-121.

Sidanius, T., Pratto, F., van Laar, C., & Levin, S. (2004). Social dominance theory: Its

agenda and method. *Political Psychology, 25*(6), 845-880 Retrieved from

http://www.jstor.org/stable/3792281

St. Mary's College of California. (n.d.). Handing conflict within an academic setting.

Retrieved from http://www.stmarys-ca.edu/node/8554

Stonehill College. (2012). Stonehill College: Office of Intercultural Affairs Workshop

Offerings. Retrieved from http://www.stonehill.edu/x19528.xml

Torraco, R. J. (2008). Preparation of midskilled work and continuous learning in nine

community college occupational programs. *Community College Review, 35*(3),

208-236.

United States Department of Labor. (2008). *National compensation survey: Occupational

earnings in the United States, 2007*. Retrieved from

http://www.bls.gov/ncs/ncswage2007.htm

Wassmer, R., Moore, C., & Shulock, N. (2004). Effect of racial/ethnic composition on

transfer rates in community colleges: Implications for policy and practice.

Research in Higher Education, 45(6), 651-672. Retrieved from

http://www.jstor.org/stable/40197365

What are T-tests for independent and paired samples. (2008). Retrieved from

http://statistics-help-for-

students.com/What_are_T_Tests_for_independent_and_paired_samples.htm

Zoomerang.com. (2012a). *Conflict dynamic profile-pilot study results.* Retrieved from

http://app.zoomerang.com/Report/ResultsPage.aspx?qn=1

Zoomerang.com. (2012b). *Conflict dynamic profile nationwide study results.* Retrieved

from http://app.zoomerang.com/Report/ResultsPage.aspx?qn=1

Zwerling, L. (1976). *Second best: The crisis of the community college.* New York:

McGraw-Hill Book Company.

Appendix A:
Conflict Dynamics Profile Sample Report for Individual Respondents *(page 1 of 8)*

conflict dynamics profile®

Individual Version
Feedback Report

Sal Capobianco, Ph.D.   Mark Davis, Ph.D.   Linda Kraus, Ph.D.

Prepared for:
PAT SAMPLE
January 5, 2011

conflict dynamics profile*

Individual Version
Feedback Report

Sal Capobianco, Ph.D.   Mark Davis, Ph.D.   Linda Kraus, Ph.D.

Prepared for:
PAT SAMPLE
January 5, 2011

Table of Contents

(CDP-I Sample, 2011)

Conflict Dynamics Profile Sample Report for Individual Respondents *(page 3 of 8)*

Introduction

Conflict refers to any situation in which people have incompatible interests, goals, principles, or feelings. This is, of course, a broad definition and encompasses many different situations. A conflict could arise, for instance, over a long-standing set of issues, a difference of opinion about strategy or tactics in the accomplishment of some business goal, incompatible beliefs, competition for resources, and so on. Conflicts can also result when one person acts in a way that another individual sees as insensitive, thoughtless, or rude. A conflict, in short, can result from anything that places you and another person in opposition to one another.

Thus, conflict in life is inevitable. Despite our best efforts to prevent it, we inevitably find ourselves in disagreements with other people at times. This is not, however, necessarily bad. Some kinds of conflict can be productive--differing points of view can lead to creative solutions to problems. What largely separates useful conflict from destructive conflict is how the individuals respond when the conflict occurs. Thus, while conflict itself is inevitable, ineffective and harmful responses to conflict can be avoided, and effective and beneficial responses to conflict can be learned. That proposition is at the heart of the Conflict Dynamics Profile (CDP) Feedback Report you have received.

Some responses to conflict, whether occurring at its earliest stages or after it develops, can be thought of as constructive responses. That is, these responses have the effect of not escalating the conflict further. They tend to reduce the tension and keep the conflict focused on ideas, rather than personalities. Destructive responses, on the other hand, tend to make things worse--they do little to reduce the conflict, and allow it to remain focused on personalities. If conflict can be thought of as a fire, then constructive responses help to put the fire out, while destructive responses make the fire worse. Obviously, it is better to respond to conflict with constructive rather than destructive responses.

It is also possible to think of responses to conflict not simply as constructive or destructive, but as differing in terms of how active or passive they are. Active responses are those in which the individual takes some overt action in response to the conflict or provocation. Such responses can be either constructive or destructive--what makes them active is that they require some overt effort on the part of the individual. Passive responses, in contrast, do not require much in the way of effort from the person. Because they are passive, they primarily involve the person deciding to not take some kind of action. Again, passive responses can be either constructive or destructive--that is, they can make things better or they can make things worse.

(CDP-I Sample, 2011)

Conflict Dynamics Profile Sample Report for Individual Respondents *(page 4 of 8)*

Guide to your Feedback Report

Constructive Response Profile

Seven ways of responding to conflict that have the effect of reducing conflict which are:

Perspective Taking - putting yourself in the other person's position and trying to understand that person's point of view.

Creating Solutions - brainstorming with the other person, asking questions, and trying to create solutions to the problem.

Expressing Emotions - talking honestly with the other person and expressing your thoughts and feelings.

Reaching Out - reaching out to the other person, making the first move, and trying to make amends.

Reflective Thinking - analyzing the situation, weighing the pros and cons, and thinking about the best response.

Delay Responding - waiting things out, letting matters settle down, or taking a "time out" when emotions are running high.

Adapting - staying flexible, and trying to make the best of the situation.

Destructive Response Profile

Eight ways of responding to conflict that have the effect of escalating conflict which are:

Winning at All Costs - arguing vigorously for your own position and trying to win at all costs.

Displaying Anger - expressing anger, raising your voice, and using harsh, angry words.

Demeaning Others - laughing at the other person, ridiculing the other's ideas, and using sarcasm.

Retaliating - obstructing the other person, retaliating against the other, and trying to get revenge.

Avoiding - avoiding or ignoring the other person, and acting distant and aloof.

Yielding - giving in to the other person in order to avoid further conflict.

Hiding Emotions - concealing your true emotions even though feeling upset.

Self-Criticizing - replaying the incident over in your mind, and criticizing yourself for not handling it better.

(CDP-I Sample, 2011)

Conflict Dynamics Profile Sample Report for Individual Respondents *(page 5 of 8)*

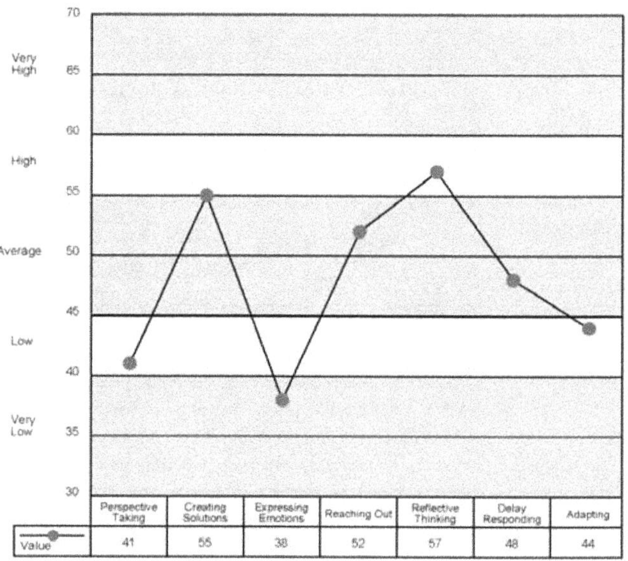

(CDP-I Sample, 2011)

Conflict Dynamics Profile Sample Report for Individual Respondents *(page 6 of 8)*

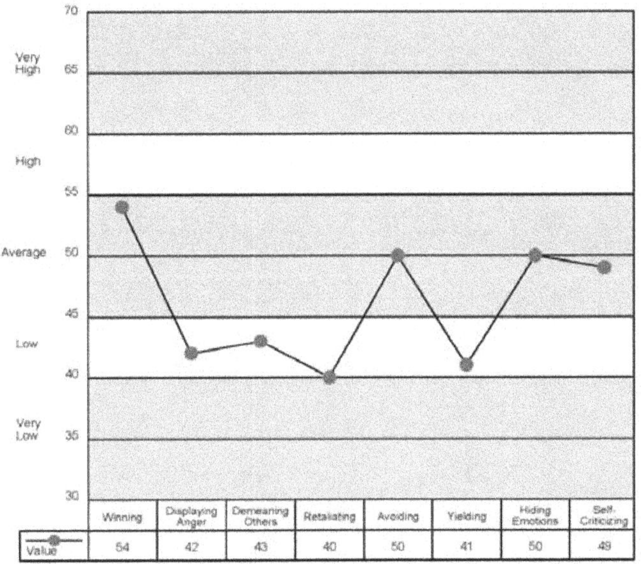

(CDP-I Sample, 2011)

Conflict Dynamics Profile Sample Report for Individual Respondents *(page 7 of 8)*

Conflict Dynamics Profile ®

Hot Buttons Profile

This portion of the Conflict Dynamics Profile Feedback Report is a bit different from the others. Instead of indicating how you typically respond to conflict situations, this section provides insight into the kinds of people and situations which are likely to upset you and potentially cause conflict to occur. In short, your hot buttons.

Below you will find a brief description of each of the hot buttons measured by the CDP, and on the following page a graph which illustrates how upsetting—compared to people in general—you find each situation. Obviously, these do not represent every possible hot button that people may have; they are simply some of the most common ones. In each case, a higher score on the scale indicates that you get especially irritated and upset by that particular situation.

Unreliable	Those who are unreliable, miss deadlines and cannot be counted on
Overly-Analytical	Those who are perfectionists, over-analyze things and focus too much on minor issues.
Unappreciative	Those who fail to give credit to other or seldom praise good performance.
Aloof	Those who isolate themselves, do not seek input from other or are hard to approach.
Micro-Managing	Those who constantly monitor and check up on the work of others.
Self-Centered	Those who are self-centered or believe they are always correct.
Abrasive	Those who are arrogant, sarcastic and abrasive.
Untrustworthy	Those who exploit others, take undeserved credit or cannot be trusted.
Hostile	Those who lose their tempers, become angry, or yell at others

(CDP-I Sample, 2011)

Conflict Dynamics Profile Sample Report for Individual Respondents *(page 8 of 8)*

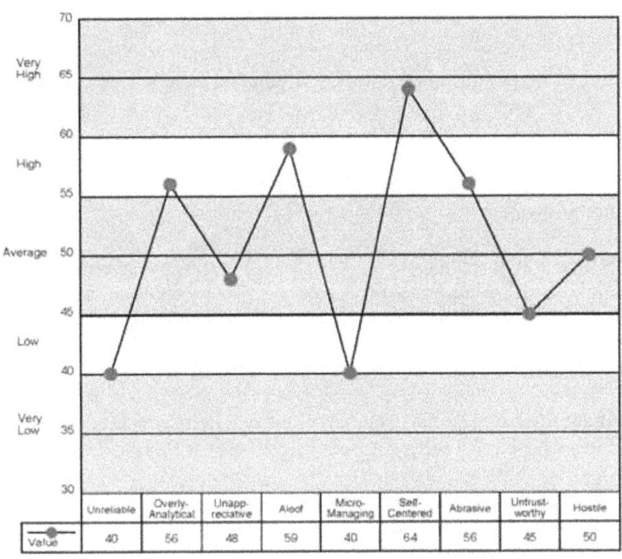

(CDP-I Sample, 2011)

Appendix B: Participation Letter

Participation Letter for Involvement in the Research Study Entitled:
"Effects of Age, Ethnicity, Gender, and Socioeconomic Background on Responses to
Conflicts among Community College Students."

Funding Source: None.
IRB protocol #:

Principal Investigator: Co-Investigator:
Ejinkonye C. Anekwe, MPA   Elena Bastidas, Ph.D
3019 Morehouse Street   3301 College Av. /Maltz Building
Columbus, Ga. 31906   Fort Lauderdale/Davie, Fl. 33314
(706) 289-9316   (954) 262-3021

For questions/concerns about your research rights, contact:
Human Research Oversight Board (Institutional Review Board or IRB)
Nova Southeastern University
(954) 262-5369/Toll Free: 866-499-0790
IRB@nsu.nova.edu

Site Information:
3019 Morehouse Street
Columbus, Ga. 31906

What is the study about?
You are invited to participate in a research study. The purpose of the study is to examine
community college students' responses to conflict based on the demographic factors of
age, ethnicity, gender, and socioeconomic background. The study seeks to provide
insight on the effects of conflict among diverse social groups of students.

Why are you asking me?
We are asking community college students between the ages of 18 and 65 to participate in the study. We are asking 150 random community college students to participate nationwide.

What will I be doing if I agree to be in the study?
You will use Zoomerang to answer a 99-question survey called the Conflict Dynamic Profile-Individual, or CDP-I. The questions will pertain to individual responses to various conflict scenarios. The estimated time to complete the survey is 15 minutes. If you agree to participate in the survey, you will be asked to enter demographic information concerning your age, gender, ethnicity, and socioeconomic background.

Is there any audio or video recording?
The survey will not be subject to audio or video recording.

What are the dangers to me?
The risks to you are minimal and may be no greater than the risks you face every day. By filling out the survey on conflict dynamic profile, you may recall bad experiences you must have had dealing with conflict. If you have any questions regarding the research, your research rights, or have a research-related injury, please contact Ejinkonye Anekwe, the principal investigator, at 706-289-9316. You may also contact the IRB at the numbers indicated above with questions as to your research rights.

Are there any benefits for taking part in this research study?
There are no benefits for taking part in this study.

Will I get paid for being in the study? Will it cost me anything?
There are no costs to you or payments made for participating in this study.

How will you keep my information private?
The researcher will not have information about identity of subjects at all during the process. You are not required to include your name or any other forms of identification in the survey at all. In addition, Zoomerang does not provide the researcher with any information about participants at all, e.g. emails, names, IP numbers, or any other form of identification. The researcher will keep all survey results in a password-protected computer and maintain the data for 36 months from the conclusion of the study. Afterwards, the researcher will destroy all the data in order to ensure your confidentiality and privacy.

Use of Student/Academic Information:
Student and academic information data will not be used in this study.

What if I do not want to participate or I want to leave the study?
You have the right to refuse participation in the study by not filling out the survey. You will not be penalized for refusing to participate.

Voluntary Consent by Participant:
By clicking on the Agree button below, you indicate that this study has been explained to you

> You have read this document or it has been read to you
>
> Your questions about this research study have been answered
>
> You have been told that you may ask the researchers any study related questions in the future or contact them in the event of a research-related injury
>
> You have been told that you may ask Institutional Review Board (IRB) personnel questions about your study rights
>
> You are entitled to a copy of this form after you have read and signed it
>
> You voluntarily agree to participate in the study entitled "Effects of Age, Ethnicity, Gender, and Socioeconomic Background on Responses to Conflicts among Community College Students."

Please click AGREE if you consent to involvement in the study. You will be directed to the CDP-I questionnaire. Click DISAGREE to be directed away from this page. Thank you for taking the time to read the participation letter.

Appendix C: Demographic Survey

Please answer the following demographic questions below. Afterwards, click on the NEXT button to start taking the survey.

1. How old are you?
______ Years

2. Choose the gender that you belong to.
A. Female B. Male C. Other

3. Please select one of the following ethnic groups to which you belong.
A. African-American B. European-American (Non-Hispanic) C. Hispanic
D. Asian/Pacific Islander E. Alaskan Native/Native-American F. Two or more ethnicities G. Other ethnicity

4. Select the socioeconomic background (annual family income) to which you belong.
A. Up to $9,999 year   B. $10,000-$19,999 a year C. $20,000-$29,999 a year   D. $30,000-$39,999 year   E. $40,000-$49,999   F. $50,000-$59,999   G. $60,000 and above

Appendix D: Screening Page

Before you continue with the survey, make sure that the following information applies to you.

Are you a community college student?
A. Yes
B. No

If the information applies to you, click NEXT to continue. If not, then DO NOT continue with the survey. Thank you.